Diva

Diva

The Life and Death of Maria Callas
Steven Linakis

Peter Owen · London

ISBN 0 7206 0578 4

To Litza and Jackie

PETER OWEN LIMITED
73 Kenway Road London SW5 0RE

First published in Great Britain 1981
© 1980 by Steven Linakis

Printed and bound in Great Britain by Redwood Burn Ltd
Trowbridge and Esher

A241210424 Ⓜ

Contents

Author's Note

Contrary to what one might think, it was not always very pleasant to be related to Maria Callas. I would rarely, if ever, mention it. It was not that I disliked Maria nor was I ashamed of her. Quite the opposite was true. But I always knew exactly what I was in for.

Tebaldi's fans, then later Sutherland's, would land on me at a gathering, figuratively pinning me to the wall, and they would tell me with great delight just how wobbly and strident Callas' voice was on the high notes, making comparisons with known divas and others I had never even heard of.

Or there were those who felt compelled to tell me all the gossip as gospel, which was usually so distorted and magnified that it was downright ludicrous. Rarely was the talk about Maria's many accomplishments, but rather about her many antics, imagined or otherwise. Or there were those who would delight in telling me just how ugly they thought she was. Or, "The nut who's always getting her pan in the papers." And she was once vilely described as having "two big eyes like [obscenities] in the snow."

Maria may never have heard any of these things (I think she might have killed those people if she had). Still, this was the "popular opinion" about her. I suppose it was all a spill-over from the voluminous articles and newspaper reports published during her lifetime, many of which were as inaccurate and as vicious as the cocktail-party gossip.

viii

Even though I have long thought of doing this biography of Maria—for nearly twenty years, in fact—when the time actually came for me to write it, I was very reluctant to do so. I would rather have dealt with the subject of World War II and the Mafia, which I have already done, literally at the risk of my own life. I felt that Maria should be left in peace. But there have been over a dozen biographies of Maria, of one sort or another, and more are on the way. In most instances, I found the same discrepancies and inaccuracies, the same old fables repeated over and over again.

One biographer, however, has written a marvelous history of her art, and some of the books are pictorially quite beautiful. What was sorely lacking, as far as I was concerned, was an overall sense of what Maria was really like—an understanding of her as a human being. So I wasn't merely out to join the parade. My hope was to set the record straight, finally bring understanding to Maria's memory, and explain how all of her actions actually contributed to her art.

I am embarrassed to say—and I do so only at the insistence of my editor whom I have known for all of seventeen years—that I have total recall—to a point that sometimes it is quite painful. I not only remember what was said, but *how* it was said. There are a number of people who wish I didn't remember quite as well. However, I am required to say that the dialogue contained herein is presented exactly the way I remember it, without additions or subtractions. At other times, I have had to draw from the sources themselves: Maria and particularly her mother were very good storytellers. Only in rare instances did I have to depend on outside sources, and on those occasions I went to a great deal of trouble to ensure accuracy. Beyond that, I have not taken any liberties, or author's license, although at times it was very tempting.

Lastly, I would like to express my gratitude, affection, and love to Maria's sister, Jackie, and her mother, Litza. This book would not have been possible without them.

S. L.

"Who rides atop the tiger can never get off."
A Chinese proverb.

Prologue

I had sadly read how Mary collapsed to the floor of her Paris apartment and was helped to her bed, where she died on September 16, 1977. Mary, whom everyone didn't know, was Maria Callas.

The night of her death became for me a private eulogy of remembrance—before her rise, before anything. I remembered the years I lived with her family when she was a young girl with heavy glasses and pimples, and her singing "La Paloma" with what no one then could have assessed as a great voice—contrary to what her mother might have said. This was before her unofficial debut on the "Major Bowes' Amateur Hour." I remembered the time she was singing, accompanying herself at the family's pianola, an old clunker, and afterwards I had asked her, "Who do you think you are? Grace Moore?" She answered, "Better. Much, much better."

I thought of all that had happened after she arrived in Athens with her mother, caught not only in World War II but also in the Greek Civil War, and of what really happened when she returned to the States, and some of it downright funny, such as when she was nearly arrested for assaulting her father's mistress. It was then that I discovered for myself what an incredibly fine actress she was. And I remembered that her voice was never better than in '47, contrary to what Eddie Bagarozy, Louise Caselotti, and the director of the old Met had said. At least I thought so.

3

She could belt out huge chest tones and incredible trills, and hit high E-flats that made the windows shake and the dogs howl. Metallic or not, hers was a unique voice that took some getting used to. And the reality, the truth, the brutal snobbery and rejection she had to endure at the hands of the late Edward Johnson, who was then director of the old Met, and what she swore to do and did, were experiences that in many ways accounted for many of her difficulties.

I remembered the very beginning of her rise and her extraordinary courage; the break with her mother, Litza, which had to be as painful as performing an appendectomy on oneself; and then, years later, when her mother almost went on welfare and I had become the mediator with Onassis, before the official mediator was named—Dr. Lantzounis, who had brought Maria into the world.

All that I remembered, and much more. We weren't just related, but close friends, then finally enemies, at least as far as Maria was concerned. But I am sure now that it didn't end that way when I recall the very last time I saw her.

That was back in March of '72, when she was about to conclude her master's classes at the Juilliard School of Music in New York City. I had received what I first thought was a wrong number. Then someone was calling for Maria's mother when a man's voice with a slight accent asked, "Mr. Papadopoulos? Someone wishes to speak to you."

"You've got the wrong number."

"No, no. Madame Callas wishes to speak to you."

"Litza?" I asked.

"No, sir. Maria Callas."

"You kidding? *Who* is this?"

Then another voice—Maria's. I hadn't heard from her in years, not since our last encounter aboard the yacht *Christina*, a meeting which had raised more questions than it had answered as far as I was concerned. Now Maria wasn't nearly as high-sounding as I once remembered. She seemed more like a total stranger. But it was Maria, all right, shy and vulnerable one moment, then tough as hell the next. She asked to see me as soon as possible, within the hour, and to tell no one, especially her mother's lunatic friends. "Something very important," she said.

"What's so important?" I asked.

"Look, you, just get over here and I'll tell you."

"Well, I can't just come this minute."

"Oh, forget it."

"Wait a minute. Of course I want to see you. All right. But don't you have to be at Juilliard tonight?"

"Not tonight," she said. "I'm sick."

"All right. What time is it now? Five? How about if I come by at eight? But where the hell are you?"

"Plaza Hotel. Be here at eight. I'll expect you." She sounded anxious and rough, but then did a complete turnabout, which wasn't very surprising for her, and sounded almost amused when she added, "Mr. Papadopoulos." Before I could ask about the ridiculous pseudonym, the same man with the accent asked from what direction I would be coming. I told him I would be coming from Astoria and that I knew where the Plaza was. Still, I had no idea why Maria wanted to see me, of all people, especially after that last meeting with her and Onassis and after I had written her a blistering letter as a result of it.

When I arrived at her suite, I heard the rush of a piano at triple *forte* as the door opened. A woman, either her secretary or her maid, backed away, letting me in. She was shaken and white. Flowers, torn and ripped to pieces, were strewn all over the huge room, all over everything. Petals clung to the sheer curtains at the wide windows. Maria was at the grand piano, socking in bravura, Lisztian octaves. At another time, an earlier time, I might have asked her if she thought she was Horowitz. But no one had to tell me that she was frustrated. She would always take it out on the piano when she couldn't get something with her voice. She was ripping into the piano. It was roaring.

Then she stopped abruptly, squinting at me. The woman announced me timidly as Mr. Papadopoulos. Badly myopic, Maria took her heavy glasses from the music rack. "Oh," she said, studying me coldly before she told the woman, "No calls. Tell everyone I'm sick. And no flowers, especially from that baboon. Can you at least remember that?"

The woman almost started to cry. I felt sorry for her. I also wondered if Onassis was the baboon.

Just as the woman left, Maria said, "Stupid. You can't say

anything to anyone without them breaking into hysterics. *I'm* the one who's supposed to be so temperamental." She kissed me coldly on one cheek, then the other. "Sit, sit," she said.

I was looking around. "Love your floral arrangements," I said, "What's all this with Papadopoulos?"

"Would you rather I told everyone you were my mother's lover?"

"What?"

"Oh, sit down. Why do you have to look as though you'll explode?"

"After that? What the hell do you think?"

Seated at the sofa across from me, she suddenly smiled widely, arranging her dress with an airy manner, smoothing it out across her knees, flicking off an imaginary something with her balled handkerchief. I remember how she sometimes liked to tease me. I also remembered her being so fat and pillowy that she practically would have taken up half the sofa. Now she was tall and shapely, her reddish tinted hair tossed high, making her appear even taller. "So, Stephenaki," she said, "it's been quite a few years, too many years."

I was still incensed. "What's this about your mother and me?"

"Well, Mother preferred you to me, didn't she? I've always wondered if you had taken the place of my dead brother."

"Come on. You really don't believe that."

"Of course not. It's just that when you were interfering I told everyone I'd never heard of you, that you were probably one of my mother's lovers, that's all."

"That's all? That's really nice."

"Isn't it? Look, you, I haven't forgotten a thing, not a goddamned thing about you, that lunatic mother of mine, and what the two of you tried to pull."

She was talking about the time her mother was about to walk into a welfare station with a battery of reporters, and I had asked Litza to hold off until I could discuss it with Maria. I had to wire Onassis finally.

"And I haven't forgotten that really rotten letter you sent me," she said.

"But it got results. It saved your neck."

"Did it? And I suppose you know what my dear mother is

pulling next. My dear, loving, lunatic mother is writing a sequel to her novel, all the finishing touches about her loving daughter. You know about it, don't you? Well, don't you?"

"I haven't heard anything like that."

"Oh, come off it. She still writes you, doesn't she?"

"Not for years."

"Don't give me that."

"Honestly. She hasn't. If I write, she writes."

"But she did write you frequently."

"Fairly."

"Still thinks the world of you, doesn't she? Would tell you everything? Well, wouldn't she?"

"Well, nearly."

"And wouldn't she give you all those interesting tidbits? And what she's going to put into that goddamned book?"

I was hesitant. "Probably. Who told you she was rewriting her book?"

"Well, isn't she?"

"I told you. I haven't heard a thing."

"Of all times to happen."

"Why should that bother you now? It's all over with."

"No, nothing's ever over with."

"Worried about all the warts?"

"Don't talk nonsense."

"Ever read her book?"

"Bah!"

"Must have read it, knowing you. You devoured it, drank it up like a sponge. Might interest you to know that her publisher was deathly afraid they would be hit with a lawsuit, and you would have been, too. So a lot was watered down. The book hardly even mentions a certain party by name. I'm sure you know who I mean." I looked around again at all the petals and torn stems. "He likes to send lots and lots of flowers. Lots of things were missing out of that book when you know most of it."

"Yes, the truth."

"And what's that? You came off as a tepid demon is all. The newspapers have done a better job on you than that. They really raked you over. Your mother? Well, mainly she told everyone how much she still loved you."

"Used me, you mean."

"Really?"

"Yes, really."

"Maria—you know I'm still not used to calling you that. But, Mary, do you really believe your mother used you? She was proud of you. She did her best for you. She wasn't a stage mother, the way you've gotten it around. Not in those terms."

"No?"

"Not from what I saw. And I saw quite a bit. Oh, she was excitable, and it's no wonder you are. And she could be rough at times. But that doesn't mean she didn't love you, or she used you. I can think of a lot more people who did that. The one who likes to send flowers. Your career was up on a shelf. You were his private property. You couldn't have liked that very much."

"You really don't know, do you? I thought you would understand."

"I do."

"No, you never understood what was happening." She said nothing else. She went to the window, crossing her arms tightly. Finally, she said, "There should be a law." She fell silent again, taking deep breaths, her arms crossed even tighter. Then she told me, "You know, my career was just for the money. Don't you see that? Mother was going to be the grand lady while I had to keep shoveling it out, screaming my guts out to get it. Well, nobody lasts in this business. Nobody. She always kept after me until I was nothing more than a goddamned singing machine making money. Tell me, was I so dreadful in the beginning? Tell me. For God's sakes, tell me."

"No, you weren't. You really weren't."

"You know how it was. I've never said anything, not really, while she kept blabbing to all the newspapers. If I'd said anything, anything that was the real truth, who would have believed me? I'd have thrown her out. She'd still be the poor suffering mother of *La Diva*. Well, it wasn't like that in the war. That lousy war and the rest of it."

"Listen, Mary, a lot of people did lousy things in the war. They had to. That was the way it was."

"Oh, yes, the way it was. What do you know about it? You were in America."

"The hell I was. I was in the war, all the way in it."

"So were we all. There's no point talking about it. What's the sense? She'll still tell her marvelous story. Such a tragic story."

"Listen, I really doubt that your mother is doing anything. You're still sending her money, aren't you?"

"Always the money. Steve, I just can't have another problem from her, not now. I'm seriously considering starting my career again."

I looked at her. It was more than a rumor that her voice was gone. "Well, in that case," I said, "I'd better write her and find out. I'm sure there's nothing to it. I'm sure she's not planning anything like that. She wouldn't risk it. Why don't you ask her straight out?"

She said nothing.

"All right," I said. "I'll find out. I'll write her tonight."

"And let me know. I have to know. I just can't have anything going wrong now."

Her enormous eyes were going even wider. This time she kissed me warmly on both cheeks, sighed, and said, "Now, I feel much better." Then she kissed me again, more affectionately, but her hands and chin were quivering.

Then she spoke about a number of other things, as though she had the need to get away from all that with her mother and Onassis. I tried to lighten the situation by telling her I had gotten a counterfeit pass to see her at Juilliard, but I was afraid of getting caught.

"You? Afraid?" she said.

"Not really." Then I told her how I tried to see her perform every chance I got when she was in New York, how I had to deal with all sorts of shady characters to get tickets and how for her première at the Met I had a lousy seat behind a pole. The situation was lightened, all right.

"So what happens now that you're leaving Juilliard?" I asked.

"Ha! I'm never going back, I can tell you. Not to that circus."

Still, her dilemma with her mother, the way she saw it, was very apparent. She had some biting things to say about Onassis, that *vlahos*, that peasant, reminding me that I had some idea what she was talking about when he skipped the country to avoid paying the settlement he had promised for her mother. That had been when Onassis suggested a villa and $1,000 a month for Litza rather than having her go on welfare. This was the first time I had learned that it was *his* idea to slip out of the agreement and that all along Maria thought he had made the arrangements with Litza.

"So that's what happened," I said.

"Of course, that's what happened." She still had some biting things to say, how he had shelved her, wasted her talent all those years, pinning her to his butterfly collection, as he had Jackie Kennedy. "The very best hell money could buy," she said.

I began to feel that I understood her finally, at least as far as Onassis was concerned. She needed something as big as her career, and Onassis, despite all reports, had proved a very poor substitute.

When I was about to leave, she told me, "Call me the moment you know anything. I have to know." Then she kissed me warmly again. "*Adio*," she said.

I had no idea that this would be the very last time I would ever see her.

The significance of the name Papadopoulos didn't occur to me until days afterward. During the war, that had been the code name the BBC used for a Scots airman named John Atkinson who had been killed. I suppose, part of what made Maria run had been the war.

Book One

One

❧

There is some minor controversy surrounding Maria's birth as to the date and even the weather. The date of her birth is given officially as the second of December 1923, rather than the fourth. The State Department people, who can be sticklers about such things, particularly on issuing a passport, have it down as the second, while her mother has it as the fourth. Publicly, her mother has stated that she was born during a storm, the worst snowstorm she had ever seen. Privately, it was a clear, fine day. Symbolically, it would seem that Maria was the product of two extremes, the Deity and the Devil.

In Flower Hospital in Manhattan, Maria was born nameless. Her mother, Litza, did not want her. Litza had lost her three-year-old son, Vacily, in a typhoid epidemic just months before in Greece. She wanted another son, just like her Vacily. So a name had to be picked at random for the bead bracelet. The nurse was told to call the baby Sophia. Litza didn't care.

Maria was finally christened three years later as Cecilia Sophia Anna Maria Kalogeropoulos. Kalogeropoulos, which means "The Good Brother," was legally changed to Callas soon afterward, because it seemed that no one but a Greek could pronounce it. Maria was called Mary by the family. I have been told she was called Mary Anna and that she preferred it, but I don't remember that at all. She did use a number of names as though she was trying to decide who she wanted to be.

Her family lived for a time in Astoria, Queens, near or on Ditmars Boulevard. Most of her early years were spent in Washington Heights in upper Manhattan, where her father, George, ran his drugstore on 139th Street and Eighth Avenue.

I don't remember the time when Maria was nearly killed, except for what I have heard. She was then five, and she and her parents had just come out of their apartment building to meet her older sister, Jackie.

When Maria saw Jackie waiting to cross the street, she pulled away from her mother. A car dragged her all of twenty feet. Maria was in a coma for nearly three weeks. Her mother's account is that when she came out of the coma she spoke roughly to her mother and the rest of the family. Maria did tell me years later, "I knew what it was to die."

Even though I was seven months older than Maria, I can't very well evaluate, or even remember, very much of what was going on during those very early years. I vaguely recall playing with Maria, or Mary, under the dining-room table and seeing all sorts of people over for Sunday dinners. Or were they parties? She was a plump little black-haired girl with huge eyes and round face, going to the pianola every chance she got, drawn like a magnet. She sounded like a bird chirping, like Stephenakos, the canary, when she sang along with the piano roll. Later she seemed to be imitating her sister, Jackie.

Well into the Depression years, my own mother separated from my father and had to work twelve hours a day, often longer, beading dresses. Since I was an only child and had to be left alone, Litza insisted that I come live with her family. If I had been older at the time, I might have wondered. Litza, after all, was a Dimitroadis and very proud of her family background, while my mother was just a Kalogeropoulos. But it seemed that Litza wanted me to live with them more than George did, and I stayed until they left for Greece. So I saw what was happening, though I didn't fully understand it at the time.

Litza and George argued constantly. Litza was a warm, loving woman, although I was too young to appreciate just how attractive and charming she was. But she had a devilish temper, calling her husband a *zo* and *vlahos*—an animal and a peasant, in that order—reminding him of her distinguished background, of a grandfather who was a commander in the Balkan War, and of her father, a colonel, who didn't want her to marry George, and how she regretted the day she ever married him and later bore him three lovely children. Whenever they argued, Maria would say, "There they go again."

The arguments had nothing to do with the crash of '29 or the fact that George had lost his drugstore and had to go on the road as a salesman for a pharmaceutical outfit, causing him to be away a good deal of the time. Partly it was that George liked the opposite sex a bit too much. If he wasn't shouldering someone at the dinner table or playing kneesie, he would ball bread to the size of a pea and aim it for the deep cleft of a woman's breasts. On the other hand, he was violently jealous of Litza.

He would never allow her to pass the time of day with any of his male friends. She was only to bring them coffee and cook his meals. He was very repressive and quite typical of some Greek males. Litza had far too much character to allow that sort of thing, and in many ways she was a forerunner of the Women's Liberation Movement, at least with regard to having her own identity. So Litza and George always argued.

Litza told me of the time before the stock market crash when she worked as a cashier in George's drugstore. All that really happened, and I can believe her, was that a good-looking man spoke to her about the weather, saying it was a beautiful day. All Litza had answered was, "Yes, isn't it?"

George went into a tantrum, and then Litza outdid him, screaming that he could do whatever he wanted with women, even in front of the children, but that she couldn't even say good morning to a man. After throwing the big ledger at him, she rushed over to the poison cabinet and took out a bottle of belladonna without realizing what it was, emptying out a handful of pills and swallowing them. She was unconscious when an ambulance rushed her to Bellevue Hospital.

Days later, a Greek doctor admonished her, "You Greek women are slaves to convention. Why do you put up with all this?"

Litza gave the only answer she knew: "My children."

Some of the main arguments I recall had to do with piano lessons for the two girls. George thought it idiotic to spend his hard-earned money on such nonsense when people were selling apples in the streets just to survive. He called Litza a lunatic when she threatened to take her own life, and he would ask, "Is your life less important than piano lessons?" He felt it was insane, ludicrous, absurd. But Litza was so determined that she won out and the girl's first teacher was Signorina Santrina. It was too much for my uncle when Litza wanted both girls to have voice lessons as well. He absolutely wasn't having any of that.

Both girls loved Rosa Ponselle. For hours on end, they would listen to scratchy shellac recordings of Ponselle, often the same record was played again and again. It was boring as hell. And both girls, I thought, made themselves silly singing along with Ponselle. Or they would fight to get to the piano first, and there was a constant bickering about whose turn it was to play. Snatches of arias, short pieces, Czerny and Hanon exercises would be heard until eleven at night, and every night. And although I was beginning to get interested in the piano, I could never have gotten to the piano even if I wanted to.

Jackie was then sixteen, and Maria only ten, but Maria was far more assertive. I couldn't appreciate that they really were two aspiring divas in embryo. I thought Jackie's voice was better and Maria's thinner. It was certainly not the vocal equipment she had in later years. In fact, it did not resemble her mature voice at all. And I should remember it, having heard it often enough. The only one who was sure she had a golden voice, even before it had asserted itself, was her mother.

I have heard stories of how Litza pushed Maria and how Maria was the by-product, particularly in her shortcomings, of a stage mother. Maria may have gone to her grave believing it, but Litza's only crime, if it was then a crime, was to do everything she could for her daughters and start them each off with the same opportunities and the same repertory. My own view is that Litza simply had enormous pride and belief in her daughters and that Maria would never have done anything she didn't want to do.

Maria would sing at the drop of a hat. She sang for public-school events at every opportunity and even once sang down to the street, where a crowd gathered. No one beat her or put her in bondage to sing on the "Major Bowes' Amateur Hour." You couldn't have kept her away. I am almost sure it was her own idea to use the ludicrous stage name of "Anita Duval," which to me sounded more appropriate for burlesque. I believe she did appear under the name of "Nina Foresti" although I know she won the show's first prize, a Bulova watch.

I have also heard that Maria had a miserable early life. Or that all the bickering and arguing between Litza and George had something to do with it. That's ridiculous. If anyone was affected, it was Jackie. Maria would laugh at it all. I seriously doubt Maria knew or sensed that her mother had preferred to have a boy when she was born. She did believe herself to be a fat, ugly duckling, and thought that Jackie was preferred over her, which may have been why she was so assertive, precocious, competitive, and even a bit of a tomboy.

Once when we both were about twelve years old, Maria said it was her turn on roller skates. I had made the mistake of telling her it was my turn. She knocked me over, yanking the skates right off my feet. The corner of my mouth was split open, and later I had to have three stitches. She wasn't in the least sorry. It had been my own fault. It had been her turn.

Another time, I had fallen off a backyard fence. She let me lay there and wouldn't do anything, although I knew my arm was broken. I had to promise not to say it was her fault. I would have promised her anything, and I had to swear it before she went to get her mother.

Her mother used to draw out a cold by heating up glass cups with candles and putting them all over your chest or back. Maria would never whimper or complain. The cups slurped and popped when they were pulled off, leaving red marks like rising cupcakes. It hurt like hell and I would rather have had the cold. God, how I hated it. Maria would always tell me to stop complaining.

Her mother liked to tell everyone that Maria's voice came from Litza's side of the family. Litza's father, Petros Dimitroadis, loved Italian arias, and though he never had a music lesson in his life, he was always singing. Litza told me that once an Italian tenor came to their village to give a concert, and when the tenor heard Petros sing he gave back all the money paid for the concert, went back to his room, and shut himself in. Petros, he said, sang better than he did.

There was no doubt that Litza, stage mother or not, had a sweet obsession for Maria. Vocal lessons were too expensive in New York. George argued he was not wasting another nickel on such idiotic nonsense when nothing would come of it, and that he would rather put his savings toward buying back his drugstore. The only remedy for Litza was to take the girls to Athens with the vague hope that her own family would contribute toward Maria's training.

Late in 1937, Jackie, who was then nineteen, went alone to Greece. A few months later Maria and her mother followed aboard the S.S. *Saturnia*. George may have been relieved, but I felt very sorry and sad when they sailed away. All they had was their luggage and their three canaries.

After they arrived in Athens, they wrote frequently, saying that Litza was a lousy sailor, seasick throughout the voyage, while Maria bored everyone at a ship's party singing "Ave Maria," "La Paloma," and the "Habanera." "Greece," she wrote, "is a funny place. They all speak Greek. Ha, ha."

Maria wrote that she lived with her grandmother and many relatives, not far from the Acropolis. Litza's brother, Efthemios, was far more impressed with Maria's voice than with Jackie's. "Ha, ha," she added. Efthemios promised to arrange for an audition at the Conservatory of Ethnikon. Litza had some other relatives, very rich from an olive oil business, but they were too snobbish and wouldn't have anything to do with helping Maria.

Within a month, the girls and their mother moved to Therma Patission, a very old and very cold house in which it was sometimes too cold for Maria to practice. They moved to a far better place at Patission 61, where Maria wrote that they were getting up in the world—" . . . the top floor. It's much nicer than father's." The building had an elevator and a porter, and the family even had a cook named Athena and a maid's room, but the maids didn't sleep in. The room was used for the canaries. In many ways, life was far better there than in America, which was supposed to have so many opportunities, including its streets paved with pure gold. "Why," Maria asked, "do they still teach fairy tales in American schools?"

Athens turned out to be Maria's place of opportunity, that Litza doggedly helped her pursue. First to be approached was Maria Trivella, who taught at the Conservatory of Ethnikon. Litza's brother had come through with the promised audition. He attended the audition with two of his sisters, as well as with Litza and Jackie. Litza felt that Maria sang like an opera star.

Trivella took Maria under a scholarship when no scholarships were being given to anyone under sixteen. Maria, who was thirteen and a half and big for her age, was passed off as sixteen by Litza. Litza might not have been able to afford the lessons otherwise. Though George had promised to send $100 a month, he had sent practically nothing.

For over two years, Maria studied with Trivella, who also taught her French as well as Greek since Maria spoke broken Greek with an American accent. As luck would have it, Elvira de Hidalgo, a former diva of the Metropolitan and La Scala, who had once sung with Enrico Caruso, accepted a post at the Athenon Conservatory. Soon afterwards, Maria was presented to the admissions board.

Hidalgo recalled years later that the idea of such a girl wanting to be a singer was laughable. Maria was very tall, fat, and wore thick glasses, behind them were huge but unfocused, unseeing eyes. She was ungainly with a dress too long and too large, buttoned in front and shapeless, and wore crushed sandals. She sat biting her nails while waiting her turn.

It was quite another matter when Maria went into the "Ocean" aria from Weber's *Oberon*. Hidalgo heard violent cascades of sound, though not fully controlled, filled with drama and emotion. Hidalgo imagined what a joy it would be to work with such a voice, to mold it into perfection.

This account had been in *Oggi*, the Italian magazine, and was probably true. Hidalgo did more for Maria during the next five years than Trivella, as far as helping to mold Maria into the finished diva. Maria performed not only at the Athens Royal Theater but at the ancient amphitheater of Herodes Atticus, under the enormous heights and high wall of the Acropolis, in sight of the Parthenon. And Hidalgo is credited with having introduced Maria to long-neglected works of Donizetti, Rossini, and Bellini.

Hidalgo, however, was not Maria's second mother as she later pretended to be, even though Maria herself may have given her that idea. Maria respected her and picked her brains every chance she got, but she did not like her very much. It was really Trivella who was Maria's second mother. Trivella, so short and plump, was always happy, while Hidalgo was serious and pompous as far as Maria was concerned. Maria described Hidalgo as having the huge chest of a typical old-time diva.

It has often been misstated that Maria was thirteen when

she sang the role of Santuzza in *Cavalleria Rusticana*. She was just a few weeks away from turning fifteen. Nor did the house give her a standing ovation. It was a respectful response for a student performance and no more, even though she won first prize.

Maria was the lead soprano in two student productions of Verdi's *Aïda* and *The Masked Ball*. When the basso Nicola Moscona heard her in *Aïda*, he told her mother, "Your daughter will be famous, and you will eat with a golden spoon."

Hidalgo did get Maria her first professional role. It was only a small part in Von Suppé's *Boccaccio*, as one of the four girls who sing and dance in a barrel. It seemed, though, that this was the beginning of her career.

It was also the beginning of the war.

Two

In a curious way, a performance of *Madama Butterfly* by the Athens Royal Theater seemed to go together with the start of the war. Puccini's son was invited to attend, with a formal reception to be held afterwards at the Italian Embassy. There was a display of Greek and Italian flags, and a cake bore the words *"Viva la Grecia."* During all this pomp, Italian Ambassador Grassi received secret instructions from Rome.

Almost twenty-four hours later, Grassi presented himself to Greek Prime Minister Metaxas. A nervous, stone-faced Grassi cited numerous provocations by both Greek troops and nationals, and said it was the directive of his country, more an ultimatum, that Italian troops occupy various strategic points in Greece. Greeks have never been known to take threats or ultimatums very well, Metaxas in particular, and he rejected the Italian directive. Italy had its excuse to declare war that morning. So the war that plagued much of Europe now plagued Greece. And Italy made the serious mistake of believing that it could defeat the Greeks without its Axis partner.

The Greek army was small, outnumbered, but they not only repelled the Italian invasion through Albania, they humiliatingly routed the Italians all the way back to the Florina region near the Yugoslavian border. The Italians were held in the mountains of Albania all that fall, winter, and early spring.

That spring was worrisome to the Greek high command.

Spring was ideal for the Italians to mount their offensive. The German army would have to join them in order to save them from their disgrace, however, and the German army did, invading Greece early in April '41. The city of Salonika was bombed, and its ports were devastated. Periodically, the Athens radio stations gave bulletins.

On the very same day, joined by her sister, Jackie, who was also studying at the conservatory, Maria kept her lesson with Hidalgo despite the fact that a heavy air raid seemed imminent. Litza, like everyone else, took her maid marketing to buy everything she could. She even bought food for her canaries. Within four hours, nothing was left in the markets.

Strangely, Athenian women jammed the beauty salons as though that night, when they felt a raid was sure to hit, they were all going to a ball. At Patission 61, Litza had a good meal prepared for the family, as though it might be their last. She tried to talk about war and what it could mean. She wasn't very successful. Maria would not listen to Litza. Instead Maria accompanied herself at the piano as she sang one of her standbys, "La Paloma." The raid did not come that night or any other night.

Athens fell to the Italians and the Germans on April 27. Everything stopped in the city. Stores and *tavernas* were shut tight. There was only the rhythmic crack of enemy boots in the streets, and the only Greeks were the dead and dying. The dead were like dirty discarded bundles covered with lime.

The Germans imposed a strict 6 P.M. curfew. Except for the churches, all schools and public places were closed. To continue her lessons, Maria would go to Hidalgo's house. The fear that she could be shot by a German patrol for little or no reason did not dissuade Maria. She merely changed her practice schedule to fit the curfew. To her, the war had proved an intrusion and nothing more.

One night, a Greek resistance officer with the ELAS whom Litza knew came to Patission 61. With him were two men. Even though they were in civilian clothes, one had only to look at the two to know they were not Greeks. Litza made the sign of the cross when she was asked to hide the two English airmen for a short time and was told that there was nothing to worry about.

She was beside herself, asking the officer if he was crazy. The Germans would shoot them all dead, including her and her daughters, on the spot. The Greek resistance officer assured her that she was mistaken. The Germans would take them out first, then shoot them.

"No, no, no!" Litza said. "Get them out!"

But the officer persisted. To this day, Litza cannot understand why she ever consented to hide the two airmen. A sense of patriotism had nothing to do with it. All during the time the airmen hid in the canary room, Litza worried at every knock at the door, at every step in the hall. Litza would not risk telling her closest friends, even Milton Embirikos, who was engaged to Jackie, and who helped more than anyone else during those days.

I don't think I was ever told the name of the cold Englishman with the light hair, only that Litza did not like him and trusted him less. The other, a Scot named Lieutenant John Atkinson, was dark and a bit of a comedian. He called Litza "Mama," and both girls really liked him.

The airmen would rarely venture out of the canary room, and they would never put on the light. But every night at nine they would listen to the BBC. Once Milton heard the radio turned on to the BBC, and said that it was very dangerous to listen to the forbidden station. Maria laughed at him and said they weren't even listening to it, and that it was far more interesting than some silly news about the war. Maria began to sing to change the subject. Milton was apprehensive after that, wanting to know who they were hiding and asking if they knew how very dangerous that was. No one would tell him anything, and Litza would not permit him to go to the canary room. She told him her canaries were asleep and that she didn't want them disturbed. Later, Litza was very upset with the two airmen, especially since she had warned them about the radio. If it had been anyone else but Milton, they might all have been shot.

The two had been captured in Crete by the Germans. They had escaped, making it by boat, first to Piraeus and then to Athens, where they were captured a second time, and they escaped again. But they were bored with being cooped up in the canary room, and John Atkinson felt they were due for an airing. The

Englishman agreed, saying, "Right. A bit of a walk will do nicely."

It was bad enough that Litza worried every day, but now the "short time" for their stay was turning into weeks, making it even more dangerous. The girls wanted to take pictures of the airmen to include in their photo albums and would only say "Oh, Mother" whenever Litza expressed worry. But for the men to go out in the streets, filled with Germans, and to take her daughters on a promenade was too much for Litza.

The airmen thought the idea was the most natural thing in the world, and the girls were actually pleased. Overriding Litza's objections, the girls said there was one thing they had to do first, and that was to dye the Englishman's hair black so he would pass for a Greek. The Scot didn't need it. Litza crossed herself three times in succession, as she had already done several times. The dyed, severe black hair on the Englishman looked ridiculous, discordant with his light complexion. To the girls, it didn't matter. To Litza, this wasn't merely ridiculous. This was lunacy.

Arm-in-arm, in broad daylight, the foursome walked the streets of Athens. It was a dangerous lark when they could have run into frequent German military police patrols. The girls were not even concerned about the danger. In fact, they enjoyed it.

It took all of six weeks before the two airmen were taken to another safe house. Maria and Jackie missed them as soon as they were gone, but Litza was more than glad they had finally left.

The very next day, Italian troops, at least a squad, came to their apartment, pounding on the door with pistol and rifle butts. "Open immediately!" someone shouted.

Litza made the sign of the cross three times, very rapidly, and then admitted them. She skipped away when they all rushed in, pistols and rifles at the ready. "What is it? What is wrong?" she asked.

A young officer asked, "Where are they?"

"Who?"

Troops rushed past her. Litza felt a cold chill. Even though the two airmen were gone from the canary room, there were still the photo albums and letters that could implicate her family. It would mean the deaths of Litza and her daughters.

Maria, at the piano, calmly struck a chord. She had the

squad's attention with that. Then she opened her mouth and began to sing a selection from *Tosca*. No doubt this was when
Tosca, tall candles in hand, walks over the body of Scarpia.

The young officer quieted his men with a "Shhhh!" com-
parable to that of a dowager in a box seat at the opera. At seventeen years of age, Maria literally was singing for her life. Her
mother never heard her sing better.

The squad sat in a circle around the piano, listening quietly.
When she stopped, there was a pause, then sudden applause,
and, "Brava! Brava!" The officer seemed almost ill-at-ease kissing
Maria's hand and then quietly told his men to leave, completely
forgetting why they had come.

Litza made sure to clean out everything from the canary
room before the Italians realized their mistake and came back.
They returned the following day, but only to leave macaroni,
cheese, ham, and bread on the piano. And Maria sang for them
again.

A week later, late at night, there was a knock at the door
and someone called out softly in English, "Mama, let me in," repeating it several times.

In those days, Litza, like everyone else in Athens, was very
cautious about opening her door. The visitor was Lieutenant John
Atkinson. "Idiot!" Litza said to him.

She told him in whispers that the Italians had already been
there looking for him the very day after he and the Englishman
had left, and, crossing herself, she told him it was a good thing
the soldiers had not been Germans. She did not explain it.

Atkinson said he needed a pistol where he was going and
that he and his friend were going to try to make it out. "Won't
do to meet Jerry otherwise."

"What?"

"Never mind. Do you keep a pistol handy?" he asked.

"No! God, no! We would be shot having such a thing."

He agreed with her that it was silly for him to think she had
one. But then he had come back to see Jackie. "Where is she?"

Litza didn't want to include her daughter in any of this and
told Atkinson that Jackie was sound asleep.

When he was about to leave, he kissed Litza and told her,
"Mama, I'll be back after all this is over. And I'll be back to marry

Jackie. At least I'd like to think I can. Now give me your very best wishes." And he kissed her again and left.

Litza never saw him again. Over the BBC she learned what had happened. The coded message was to "Patission," Litza's apartment. "Jean Papadopoulos" had gotten out of Athens safely. But in the Peloponnesus, where he had just reached the sea, he was intercepted by an Italian patrol. He shot and killed five Italians before he himself was killed. Jean Papadopoulos was the code name for John Atkinson.

For months, because of the conservatory's forced closing, Maria did not take part in student productions. However, there was an unusual production when she sang the role of Tosca, practically from her balcony, and an unseen Mario answered her over the Athenian rooftops.

Among the many German proclamations, there was one that also proclaimed that Athenians must be quiet, making no noise whatsoever, not even in their own homes. The girls pulled the piano over to the balcony, leaving the door and the windows wide open. Maria would accompany herself and sing, and not *sotto voce*. Whenever she sang Tosca, someone, a good distance away, sang the part of Mario. It caused people in the streets to stop and listen. This went on for some time. Maria never learned who her Mario was. Although she was later to sing with the finest tenors in the world, there was not one who could compare with this Mario.

This defiance was not confined to the Kalogeropoulos family alone. Whenever German officers came into a *taverna*, every Greek would stand and bow, being objectionably polite. Or they would ignore the Germans completely. Outside, Greeks would move out into the streets as the Germans passed. Or they would sing obscene songs that jeered the Germans.

Practically all over the city black graffiti would appear on the white buildings every morning. Most of the writing was patriotic, a call to arms, or a call for the death of that maniac Hitler. But one word that stood out among all of them was *efterria* (freedom), probably the noblest word in the Greek language. German details or civilian work crews would wash it off the walls every morning. But no amount of scrubbing seemed to wash it out completely. Puddles would run muddy black along the curbing.

In the first eighteen months of the occupation, particularly the early months, many died of starvation. In the streets, young and old begged for food. Sometimes there were Red Cross packages from America. Very often, the dried staples, especially the peas, were festered with worms. Litza would either sell or give away her wormy peas to those who had animals.

The first black market to operate was outside of the city. Litza would take a wood-burning locomotive to the farm. The train would often break down, and she would have to carry her loaded bag all the way back to Athens. Sometimes she found fresh vegetables, but more often than not her bag was filled with soggy and half-rotten greens, an occasional scrawny rabbit, and an undernourished chicken. A few times, she was lucky to get some eggs and veal. Maria went along on a few occasions. Maria never went alone, as was often quoted, to feed her family.

Afterwards, a black market began to operate in Athens. It never took very long for the supplies to be depleted, including donkey and horse meat, which Litza and the girls never touched. They could never bring themselves, no matter how hungry they became, to eat donkey or horse meat.

The main staple was a sawdust, ersatz bread. Very often, that was all they had to eat. Maria proved allergic to it, breaking out with tremendous boils which were cleared by a dermatologist who later treated the Royal Family.

If it had not been for Jackie's wealthy fiancé, Milton, the family very well might have starved to death. The food that the Italians left on the piano that one time could not have sustained them for too long. For them, though, it had been a feast.

Though their clothes began to wear out, they were used until they completely fell apart. When Milton gave Litza money to buy materials for clothing, Litza, who was always fashion conscious and a very good dressmaker, was far more concerned with durability and warmth. She knitted thick *barolas* (stockings) for the girls and herself, in addition to sweaters and scarfs. Their shoes were resoled with rubber from automobile tires. Soap, too, was scarce and was made of a gritty material that would lather to a dark gray, leaving an unclean feeling. Still, the worst thing, which none of them will ever forget, was the lack of food.

Litza would doggedly scour the city for food, and even with money it was becoming increasingly difficult to locate supplies. One day her maid, Athena, said she knew of a place to buy meat and took Litza to the poorest section of Athens.

As they stood at the door of a house, waiting a long time for someone to answer, they noticed a sickening smell. Then a dirty brute of a man stood framed in the doorway. Litza was holding a handkerchief to her mouth, covering her nose. The man obviously misunderstood her. "So," he said, "my meat is not good enough for you. You're such a lady with your *barolas* and your raggedy clothes. Come. Let me show you something."

He led them through a yard. The smell was much stronger, and what they saw sickened Litza even more. Nude human bodies were piled up like cords of wood.

"This," he told Litza, "can happen to you. You can either starve to death or eat my meat. I think you will want my meat." Then, as though it was a joke, he said he was not selling dead humans, only good beef.

Litza was so sickened that she came away without buying anything, without even looking at "the good beef." She practically ran to get away from there.

Three

$\sim$

Despite the occupation and near starvation during the first months of '41, Maria continued her private studies with Hidalgo. Ironically, if it had not been for the German *Kommandant*, all this might have come to nothing.

General Wilhelm Speidel, who commanded the German garrison of Athens, was, among other things, quite artistically and musically sensitive, and he fancied himself a patron of the arts. That summer, he ordered the 6 P.M. curfew extended to midnight and opened all the schools and theaters.

Many in the opera company of the Athens Royal Theater refused to return to the stage. They would not sing while Greece was oppressed by its conquerers. Hidalgo had practically assured Maria of prima-donna roles with the company, and it was not Maria's intentions to continue playing a nameless singer, among three others, in a barrel. She wanted principal roles so badly she could taste it. She didn't care if the Germans had tails and pitchforks, as long as she got what she wanted.

Occupation or not, war or no war, allowing nothing to get in her way, Maria resumed her studies at the conservatory, took part in student productions, and joined the remaining ranks of the Athens Royal Theater. But many sopranos with the company wanted nothing to do with the overly talented seventeen-year-old upstart, who was a favorite of Hidalgo's. Jealousies caused wrangles, and many company members were so furious with Maria that they could have killed her. Maria proved she had a better temper than all of them.

Before Maria made her first public appearance with the company, there was an unrehearsed performance in the courtyard of the Athens Royal Theater, before a small audience, in which she sang Tosca. That night, the prima donna fell ill, and Maria was given the lead. Another soprano of the repertory cast so hated Maria that she had her husband stop her at the stage entrance to keep her from singing. He told her, "You fat bitch, you're not going to pull it off. You're not going anywhere."

Maria flew at him, tore his shirt, bloodied his nose, clawed him, while he slapped and punched her about the face.

Hardly anyone of the company knew what had happened, least of all the audience crowded with German and Italian troops. Maria's first principal role was well received, although most of the applause was for the fat tenor, Antonis Thellentas, who was very popular in Athens, and who, as Maria mischievously said, wore a girdle. Maria had sung with a teary, puffy eye, and when she came home that night, it was black, shiny, and nearly closed.

The role of Leonore in Beethoven's *Fidelio* has just too many vocal and musical traps and is too taxing for a seventeen-year-old novice to pull off. Particularly for one who does not know the German language fluently, it's next to impossible. But Maria did sing Leonore at the ancient amphitheater of Herodes Atticus. What marred her performance, if it can be called that, was that she sang her role in Greek. She received her first real ovation.

A German officer got to his feet, yelling, "What an artist! What a voice! I've never heard such a Leonore!" And he proceeded to take photos of Maria like a tourist.

That same summer at the amphitheater, Maria performed the lead in a Greek opera, *Protomastorsa*, by Kalomiris. Her part was so difficult, that her voice nearly cracked. This time, it was the Greeks who gave her a standing ovation.

Athens accepted her as its own, not as an American-born singer. Her horizons—for what they were during the occupation—shifted, and she did not act the part of a novice. She was a prima donna. Whenever she performed, whether the lead or an occasional small part, she stole scenes every chance she got. She had developed such a stage presence that the rest of the company appeared to be bunglers. Whenever she stole scenes from the tenor, Thellentas, he would scream at her afterwards. But if she didn't sing up to par and Thellentas got most of the applause, she would become furious, and for her next performance she would try all the harder. And she was very critical of herself, for each and every performance, to a point that it was painful for her.

Litza would never miss a performance, and Maria would listen for her distinctive cough in the audience. If Maria did not hear it, she would complain to her for not coming. During intermissions, Litza would fan Maria with a towel, much like a fight handler, pampering her, while Maria would constantly ask what her mother thought of her voice, if it was getting better, and for Litza it always was.

The following summer, the commander of the Italian Army of Occupation directed the Athens Royal Theater to have Maria and a select troupe from the company go to Salonika to entertain the troops. Litza, who became known to the theater group as Maria's shadow, was adamantly opposed to letting Maria go unchaperoned to Salonika, which not only was at a distance, but had one of the worst reputations of all the port cities. Maria, she argued, was too young, not yet nineteen, to be exposed to such things, and too young to go alone, especially there. Litza would rather be dead than permit it.

The young Italian officer De Stasio, in charge of the operation, gave her many *bravos* for being such a good mother, but told her there was no other space allocated on the train to permit her to go along. Her reply was, "If I'm not going, neither is Maria."

The next day, quite miraculously, space was found for Litza aboard the train.

The trip was tedious, jolting to a stop all too many times. The train jolted so that they were nearly thrown from their seats, almost spilling their luggage from the racks.

For nearly a month, they stayed in Salonika at a decent hotel, enjoying meals that were normally only provided to high-ranking officers, with a choice of wine or beer to drink. It was a luxury after enduring two poor meals a day, or sometimes no meal at all.

The performances in Salonika were mainly operas in concert form, their only accompaniment being the playing of a wiry pianist who eyed all the ladies. Many of the scores were abbreviated, although this was not true for the familiar arias. When the singers were asked whether they wanted to be paid in food or money, they chorused as one, *"Food!"* On Maria's return to Athens, the Italians welcomed her back with more food.

As the long war dragged on, Maria seemed to keep totally apart from it. Despite periodic privations, she lived as though there were no occupation at all. Almost daily, she stuffed herself with all the sweets she could buy, including an ersatz ice cream.

One night, Litza met Colonel Mario Bonalti in a *taverna*. Afterwards, he came to call on Patission 61, and kept coming with food, particularly sweets for Maria. He was to Litza a very charming man and quite an accomplished pianist. He would often accompany Maria and was especially fond of her. Maria wasn't always that pleased with him. The Italian colonel's real attention was for her mother, and although Litza said they were just friends, Maria didn't like it.

Litza would have nothing to do with the Germans, unless she had to. She was shocked when a German officer sent flowers and called on Maria. It seemed that he had heard her sing Rossini's "Stabat Mater" and felt he had to meet her.

Although she was put out by all this, Litza knew that to be openly hostile risked reprisal. She awkwardly told the German officer she had nothing to offer him except a cake she could make out of chick-pea flour. "The war, such as it is," she said. He agreed with her, and he seemed embarrassed when he told her the cake would do nicely.

His name turned out to be Oskar Botman. He was twenty-four years old, and he had been badly wounded. "The war, such as it is," he said.

He was now stationed in Athens. He looked rather frail. He felt that Maria was an enchantress and was completely absorbed with her, all the while eating three slices of Litza's cake, even though she felt it was very poor. Maria became pleased with him and was very animated. Soon they all seemed to forget who he was, one of the enemy.

Maria continued to appear with the Athens Royal Theater, and in '43 she went again to Salonika, although not without her mother. But in the spring of '44 the Germans had had enough of Verdi and Puccini. In addition, Italy had surrendered to the Allies in '43. So the German *Kommandant* directed the Royal Theater Company to perform *Tiefland*, bringing about the Greek première of that opera.

Soon afterwards, d'Albert's *Tiefland* was presented with Maria as Martha. The German press was particularly impressed with the performance, describing the tenor Thellentas as widely known beyond the borders of *Greichenland*, while "Maria Kalojeropoulou" was *Greichenland's* foremost and beloved opera star.

When the soprano who had been selected for Leonore could not learn her role in time, Maria gave her second performance as Leonore in *Fidelio* during the fall of '44, but this time she sang in German. There was that majestic, vibrant finale of Beethoven's "Oh, namenlose Freude!" This was just weeks before Athens was liberated.

During the long occupation, the Greeks loathed the Italians and the Germans. The Greek resistance, the EAM and its military arm, the ELAS, were very active, especially against the Germans. German reprisals of a hundred Greeks executed for every German murdered were commonplace.

The Italian troops began to hate the Germans nearly as much as did the Greeks. The Italians had been treated like poor second cousins by the Germans, who reminded them often enough that if it hadn't been for the Germans, the Greeks would have annihilated the Italians in Albania. Then, when Italy surrendered on September 8, 1943, the surrender did not extend to the Italians occupying Greece, and the Germans called them cowards and traitors.

In the spring of '44, German troops captured all the Italian bases, herding the Italians into POW compounds and shooting those who resisted. All high-ranking Italian officers were shipped to camps in Germany. Some Greeks hid Italians, while others were able to escape to the mountains. It was during this time that Colonel Bonalti disappeared. Litza was quite sure he was dead.

Then, in early October of '44, quite unexpectedly, the war was over for the Greeks when the Germans marched north toward the Yugoslavian border. They marched away the same way they had marched into Athens, in precise formations.

The liberation was like an explosion. Constitution Square was jammed. Nothing could move. Streamers in blue and white, the colors of Greece, adorned cars and buses. Girls were kissing servicemen, Greeks, the British, and Americans. Athens was in wild jubilation, while all the church bells kept ringing and confetti floated through the air.

Litza and the girls were atop their building, tearing up German occupation money to use as confetti. The green and white fluttered down into the street. And Maria sang above it all.

Then with one war over, it seemed no time at all before the Greeks were fighting a civil war with the Communists.

On December 3, 1944, the Communists held a huge rally in Constitution Square in Athens, calling for the overthrow of the government and the abdication of the king who had deserted the Greeks in the war. When demonstrators broke through a cordon of police, the police fired on them. Within hours, Communist guerrillas had secured one square mile of the city, consisting of both Constitution and Omonia squares.

Maria and her mother, as well as a friend named Rina, were safe in their Patission apartment. But Jackie had gone to the Park Hotel, not far from Constitution Square, to have lunch with Milton. When she did not come home for days, her family was convinced she had been killed in the fighting. Only when Milton sent someone with several gold coins and a message did they know Jackie was safe with him.

For twenty days, Maria, Litza, and Rina were besieged at Patission 61. Communist guerrilla machine guns clattered over their heads on the roof. Night and day loudspeakers blared, sirens wailed amid explosions, along with rapping sheets of rifle and machine gunfire. But every day at noon the fighting would stop for an hour, as though the combatants were taking a lunch break.

For one week, Litza had a very trying guest, General John Dourendis, Greek minister of the interior. One night, he had escaped from the Communists after they scheduled him for execution. At four in the morning, the terrified general with the magnificent beard knocked at the door and asked Litza, his old friend, to hide him.

All that week the general was frightened, talked incessantly, and got in everyone's way. He made Litza so nervous that she would scream at him to stop wailing like an old woman, while Maria would yell, "Stop it! Keep quiet! Leave my mother alone! Leave us all alone!"

Then one afternoon an announcement was made over loudspeakers. At first it was barely discernible in the distance, but then echoed into the family's own street. They wouldn't dare draw the blinds. Maria carefully looked through a crack in the blinds and saw a truck with two alternately mounted loudspeakers atop its roof and crude Communist graffiti scribbled all over its body. The loudspeaker first gave off a shrill whine and then ricocheted all over the street: "Attention! Attention! Anyone found harboring Loyalist officers will be shot immediately!" The announcement was repeated again and again.

The Communist guerrillas, fierce men with coarse beards, crisscrossing bandoliers, and machine guns, didn't simply kill you. They would cut your throat and would do other vile obscenities to you if you were a man. God knew what they would do to the Kalogeropoulos family, harboring General Dourendis, the most wanted man of all. Litza simply couldn't hide him any longer. The Communists would cut her throat and Maria's. Rina said they could include her with that. So the general left just as he arrived the week before, at four in the morning.

The porter of Patission 61, a Communist, would daily write messages, appropriately in red chalk, on Litza's door to the fire escape. The messages read, "We will first kill Maria, knocking out her brains with a sledgehammer. Then we will kill Mama, then Jakinthy [Jackie]." It would be signed with a hammer and sickle.

Every morning, Maria or Litza washed the message off the door. Every morning, it would reappear. Maria was convinced that the porter was really very fond of them.

When the guerrillas ordered the porter to fight in the streets, he came scurrying back to Litza's door, begging her to hide him. And Litza did. Maria was furious with both her mother and the porter. His response was that he had been "ordered" to write the messages and that he really wasn't a very good Communist.

There was no heat and no electricity, and it was cold. For cooking fires, the family burned rags soaked in benzene. Their faces were always smudged black and greasy from the sooty smoke. The food ran out soon after the fighting began. Fortunately, Litza had saved some Red Cross packages that were sent during the occupation. Their main staple for all of those twenty days was beans. Soaked in water, they were rationed out from six to ten beans at a time.

During the fighting, the canary room was machine-gunned. It went on for a very long time. Everything was twisted, splintered, and smashed. Among the dust and hanging, shattered plaster of the smashed ceiling were the black and yellow feathers of Litza's canaries.

On two occasions, a British officer, whom Litza knew, sent a boy with a letter for her. The first time, when the boy asked for Kalogeropoulos Callas, Litza told him, "We are not Callas. Go away." She was deathly afraid that the Communists had learned about the general and were now trying to dupe them out to kill them.

But the second time, Litza admitted the boy after he explained that he had a letter from this British officer and gave the officer's name. The letter instructed Litza to put on all the clothes she could wear and to come to the British Embassy on Constitution Square.

Litza had no choice. They were facing starvation. Maria decided to risk it first, and with the boy dodged the fighting for twelve hours before she safely reached the embassy. Two days later, the boy came back for Litza and Rina. Litza wore all the blouses and sweaters she could, including three skirts and two coats. When they finally reached Constitution Square, the Greek Loyalist sentries wouldn't allow them to pass. They were suspected of hiding weapons under all the bulbous clothing. Fortunately, a British officer allowed them to pass through, taking them to British Headquarters, where they joined Maria and Jackie at the Park Hotel.

Twice the guerrillas tried to burn down the hotel, but the British succeeded in driving them off. Even though they were barricaded at the hotel and the fighting was still going on, at least Litza and her family had decent food, and for the first time in weeks they were able to wash all the soot and grime from their faces.

By February '45, Greek Loyalist and British troops managed to drive the Communists guerrillas out of Athens. There was a strained sense of normalcy until May, when the war finally ended in Europe. The Athens Royal Theater reopened, and Maria began to sing again. But she faced a new problem.

A delegation of the Royal Theater Company, who had refused to sing during the occupation, addressed the presiding government, labeling Maria as a collaborationist, citing chapter and verse how Maria sang for the enemy and fattened herself while her own countrymen starved and were murdered.

Faced with this pressure, the director of the Athens Royal Theater decided to remove Maria from the troupe until the smoke cleared.

Maria stormed when she heard this. First she was the American-born upstart. Then she was a Greek, and their queen. But then to mark her as a collaborator was too much. No doubt she was called a principal collaborator, one who gave private recitals to Hitler no less. "Bah!" she shouted. "Keep them! Keep them all! Half of these jealous so-called patriots sing off-key! The main reason, the only reason, they wouldn't sing was that the Italians would have known the difference!"

The director agreed, but he was helpless. For now, it was best if they had a parting of the ways.

"Good!" Maria said. "Perfectly fine with me! We'll have a parting of the ways, like the Red Sea!" Then she told him she didn't need his theater any longer, which was poorly lighted and too cramped on stage anyway. Singers had to do acrobatics to get around one another. Besides, she said, she had no intention of staying in Athens for the rest of her life.

Her last performance with the theater was Millöcker's *Der Bettelstudent*. In July, she decided to give a recital. The Rex Theater was loaned to her for the occasion. Maria sang arias from several Italian operas, and, defiantly, German *lieder*.

Shortly afterward, she left for New York. There was good reason. She had to.

The American Embassy had advised her that because she had come to Greece as a minor and was now an adult, she would lose her citzenship if she did not return to the States within a prescribed period of time. With all the adoration, she had never been paid very much and didn't have nearly enough money for the fare. The embassy granted her a loan which she was to repay in twenty-dollar monthly installments.

She did receive a hundred dollars from her father George,

in the first and only communication she had received from him since the start of the war. But, other than the money, the envelope contained only his address, nothing in the way of a letter. She was going to write and tell George she was coming, but the envelope with only the money irritated her. She decided not to write to him.

So in August or September of '45, when she boarded the S.S. *Stockholm* in Piraeus, she had no idea what she could expect in the States. Nor did her father know that she was coming.

Book Two

Four

~~~

In the Greek newspaper *Atlantis*, it was quite by accident that her father came across the name "Maria Kalogeropoulos" among the list of passengers aboard the S.S. *Stockholm* arriving from Piraeus. He called my mother and asked if she knew anything about it. She knew just as much as he did—nothing. George called Jimmy Zarras, a friend of mine who had known Maria as a young girl, to come along with him to the pier when the ship docked. If this really was Maria, George had no idea what she looked like as a grown woman. He felt Jimmy's eyes were better than his and that Jimmy might be able to recognize her.

The two stood waiting at the Manhattan pier, long before the white S.S. *Stockholm* with yellow markings turned into her berth and took her moorings. They watched the passengers descend the gangway and then went by the white picket fence at customs to wait for luggage inspection. Uncle George, a bit of an aged Beau Brummell with a cane and a dyed black mustache, didn't seem to be taking his usual constitution. He apprehensively kept prompting Jimmy to watch for her. It seemed a little ridiculous to Jimmy when George would walk up to a total stranger and ask, "Are you my daughter, Maria?"

He asked practically everyone he could—the ship's personnel, customs, and the passengers—if they knew a Maria Kalogeropoulos. George saw a tall Greek woman with a very broad face, moon cheeks, and black hair. She was so huge and pillowy that she practically had to sidle out from customs. He asked her, "Do you know Maria Kalogeropoulos?"

The only thing remotely familiar about the woman were her enormous eyes. This wasn't a young girl with pimples, but a woman who was nearly two hundred pounds on the hoof. She had a very broad mouth even before she smiled. "I should," she said.

It was Maria. Then they were embracing, Maria kissing her father, and he was crying. At first, she didn't even remember Jimmy Zarras. Then she said, "Oh, I remember you, Stephanaki's friend." She looked around for me until Jimmy told her I was still in the army. She was amazed and happy that her father knew she was coming. "How could you have possibly known?" she asked.

Her father told her how he had luckily come across her named listed among the passengers, while Jimmy said, "Your old man's a good detective." She was smiling but frowning at the same time. Jimmy asked, "You still speak English, I hope?"

"You ain't bird-turding," she said.

He burst out laughing. "Who the heck taught you that?"

"Some Americans. There are quite a few now in Athens."

"G.I. Joes, you mean. Cigarettes, candy, chewing gum. 'You got sister?' Hope you didn't have too much to do with them."

Even though George could speak English fairly well, during all this he repeatedly asked, "What are you two saying?" Jimmy told him it was too difficult to explain, much less translate.

In a taxi, Maria told them some of the things that happened to her. But she didn't want to talk about the war at all. She had had enough war. All she wanted now was to eat and eat. She was animated talking about a number of things, although she said very little about her career, except that she was still singing. When Jimmy asked about her mother and sister, Maria became a little irritated. "Why do you want to know about them?" she asked. "I'm here."

At her father's East 157th Street apartment, he brought out some wine. Maria began to explain how far her career had gone, and her father was surprised. He knew, of course, that she had studied, had a scholarship, and took part in student productions. But this was the first time he had heard just how far she had advanced.

"You're actually an opera singer?" George asked.

"Of course, Father. I told you."

"You're actually that good?"

"Of course I'm that good. And I'm going to be the best in the world."

"You're not serious," he said.

She got right up, threw her head back, widely opened her mouth, and hit a high note. It was ear-shattering. "That," she said, "is high E-flat. Know anyone who can do that? Or this?" And she launched into a segment of an aria that neither George nor Jimmy could identify. "There," she said.

"Well," said George, "you show improvement."

"That's all? Improvement? Ha!"

Just then, Alexandria sullenly came into the living room, wearing a housecoat. For all intents and purposes, she was George's housekeeper. When George brightly introduced her to Maria, Alexandria wouldn't even look at her and was very surly when she said, "I know who she is." George whispered something to her, hissing in her ear.

All the while, Maria was glaring. When Alexandria left, Maria asked George, "What's that?" George looked away. Then she asked Jimmy, "What *is* that?"

"What?" Jimmy said.

"That?" she said, jerking her chin in the direction that Alexandria had taken, glaring now at George.

George tried to scoff it off. "My housekeeper," he said.

"That's all? Just your housekeeper?" she asked.

George said nothing else, and he seemed very uncomfortable, awkwardly asking if she wanted more wine. She didn't want any of his wine. Then he told Jimmy, "I'm sure, my boy, that you will want more. Such a happy occasion to have Maria home again."

"I'm not home, Father," she said. "I'm just here."

She went over and fingered the piano. It was badly out of tune. She stopped. She seemed a long way away. Finally, she said she was tired from the trip, damn tired. All she wanted was to take a bath and to no longer feel the continual movement of the ship underfoot. Jimmy said he had to get going anyway. She kissed him on the cheek and thanked him for meeting her. Her father came to the door, inviting Jimmy to have Sunday dinner with them. "Yes," said Maria, "if I'm still here."

It wasn't very long afterwards that she called Jimmy Zarras, asking him if he could come over. When he arrived, she was packed, bag and baggage. She said, "Good. You're just in time to help me with my bags."

"What'samatter?" he asked.

"Ask him," she said.

George said he couldn't understand her. He asked if she had gone a little crazy.

She told him she would be staying at the Astor and that she would send him the bill. "And get this goddamned piano tuned."

Once outside, Jimmy asked, "What happened? What are you so upset about?"

She wouldn't tell him. He could only surmise that it had something to do with Alexandria. Maria told him that she wanted to get away anyway and said, "The Astor is better for what I have in mind."

"Isn't that expensive?"

"Of course. But my father will pay for it. He won't like it, but he'll pay." Then, for some reason, she spoke about me. "Why is everyone so secretive about Stephanaki?"

"What?"

"Steve. Why isn't he home yet?"

"Told you. He's still in the army."

"But the war's over."

"Maybe he likes the army," Jimmy told her, and he called her a cab. When he got her bags in, she told him to give her a call at the Astor. "Yes," Jimmy said, "but what name, Mary? Mary or Maria Kalogeropoulos, Maria Callas, what?"

"Try them all," she said.

Maria felt she would make an impression staying at the Astor, and all she had to do was present her credentials, have them listen to her, and the New York opera world would fall all over her. But she was in for a surprise.

New York has a reputation: If you can't make a living there, you can't make a living anywhere. This, however, does not apply to the arts. And New York has more than its share of talent. Artists of all shapes and sizes, be they singers, musicians, artists, or writers, are a drug on the New York market.

A singer or a musician can give a recital at Little Carnegie Hall, or any hall in the city, any time they want, provided they pay for it. All you will usually get out of it is that you'll paper the house with free tickets, and, if you're very lucky, you'll get a critic who more often that not will tear you to pieces.

It was not all that different for Maria, who promptly had the wind knocked out of her sails. No sooner had she registered at the Astor than she began making the rounds, auditioning everywhere. Among those who heard her was Giovanni Martinelli, whose voice was only a shadow of what it once was, but who was still very much a part of the opera world. Maria's main hope was that Martinelli would recommend her to the director of the Metropolitan Opera. The way I got it, Martinelli felt there were some faults between the registers of her voice and recommended further study.

Then there was Gaetano Merola, the impresario with the San Francisco Opera, who told Maria that she was still young and that she should make her career in Italy before he would sign her up. Maria told him that once she made it in Italy, she wouldn't need him any longer.

Then she sought out Nicola Moscona, the basso who was then with the Met, and who was one of the very few singers who enjoyed the benefit of being one of Arturo Toscanini's personal choices for opera roles. Moscona, who was formerly with the Athens Royal Theater, had said that Maria would become so famous that Litza would eat with a golden spoon. Maria now wanted him to recommend her to the director of the Met, as well as to get her an audition before Toscanini. Moscona told her, "Don't be ridiculous. Unknown sopranos don't ask for auditions with Toscanini." After that, Moscona ignored her completely.

Maria would try to call Moscona from the drugstore where her father worked in midtown Manhattan and Eighth Avenue. Her father's eyes would go skyward. To him all of this was a complete waste of time. Despite what she had accomplished, his opinion of her singing had changed very little since she was a young girl. The best thing for Maria, he felt, was to forget that nonsense, marry someone, preferably rich, preferably Greek, have babies, and make him a grandfather. Naturally, he said, she sang beautifully, but what good was it if she couldn't even earn a living? It was all a waste of time, he said, and he told her to forget about it. But Maria, even more determined now, wasn't forgetting anything. She didn't go through all the studies, the war, and everything else just to forget all about it.

She was still persistent about Moscona, still trying to reach him. Finally, when he would never respond to any of her calls, she became furious with him, swearing someday she would have him pay. Only afterwards did she once speak almost kindly of him. "Poor Niki," she said. Then she added some minor barbs: "So famous and not famous enough. He'll never have time for anyone else until they let him sing Méphistophélès in *Faust*."

Years later, it got around that Moscona had arranged the audition with the director of the Metropolitan. But according to Maria, it was her own persistence and determination, nothing else, that managed what was nearly impossible: an audition with the Met's director, Edward Johnson.

It also got around that Johnson had offered her the roles of Madama Butterfly and Desdemona in Verdi's *Otello*. Later it was revealed that she had been offered roles in *Butterfly* and Beethoven's *Fidelio*, but that she refused the parts because she would not sing *Fidelio* in English and she was too fat to appear as the frail Butterfly.

A newspaper quote by Edward Johnson stated, "We were very much impressed, and recognized her as a talented young woman. We offered her a contract, but she didn't like it—because of the contract, not because of the roles. She was right in turning it down—it was frankly a beginner's contract. But she was without experience, without repertory. . . ."

There wasn't any truth in Johnson's statement at all, but that was exactly the way it has been quoted over the years. The question anyone should ask was, What about all of her experience with the Athens Royal Theater? And what of her repertory from light operetta to *Tosca*, *Aïda*, and Beethoven's *Fidelio*, just to name a few? No one turns down the Met, not when you have worked to accomplish that very end. That would be exactly like saying a beginning author had turned down a half-million dollar advance. It would be ludicrous for anyone to believe Johnson.

Because of her pride and because she was so upset by the

audition, Maria would never say what had really happened when she was interviewed about it years later. The truth was known by very few, I for one knew it, and I'll get to telling the story in its proper sequence.

After the Met audition, Maria was so dejected that she felt she had to start all over again. She felt as though she had hit bottom. Through an acquaintance, she was referred to Eddie Bagarozy.

E. Richard Bagarozy, a New York attorney, managed other singers as well as his wife, Louise Caselotti, a mezzo who had succeeded in Hollywood. Maria's idea of the opera wasn't Hollywood. But she was willing to try anything.

Eddie Bagarozy liked her voice. He thought it had a very unusual range, a little tight on top, and a little rough on the bottom registers, and that her voice was unusually expressive.

Oh, he was very interested. But he told her she needed corrective studies if she ever hoped to make "the big time," and she could begin by studying with his wife. They would have an agreement whereby he would be her personal representative with the usual fee of ten percent of all gross earnings she would make. It was the usual fee, he assured her. Some managers, he said, socked a singer a lot more.

Maria was angry, not only for his critique of her voice, but because it seemed too pat a business arrangement with his wife involved as well. She only told him she would let him know, although she wanted nothing to do with him after that. But there was no one left. She had tried everyone else. She had no other choice. Some weeks later, she decided to go along with Eddie.

On hearing Maria, Louise Caselotti thought that her voice was basically a dramatic soprano, which qualified for the heaviest, most demanding roles. But it seemed that Maria's voice was harmed by her conscious lightening of it in an effort to do lyric and coloratura roles. A lot of work would be needed if Maria was to improve.

Maria, despite this, still felt that something good might come of her association with the Bagarozys. At least these people were opera *aficionados*, as well as totally sympathetic and unusually interested in her. That really mattered to Maria after so many knocks and disappointments.

After that, Maria rarely missed a lesson, working from morning until late at night. She was becoming more and more dependent on the Bagarozys, and she seemed very fond of them. But it only seemed that way.

Five

❧

I don't know exactly how long Maria was at the Astor, but it wasn't a lengthy stay. She kept sending her father the bills, and he kept ignoring them. He grudgingly paid them only after she threatened to leave the country and never see him again. After that, she was back in his apartment, and of course the piano was tuned. But things weren't going well with Alexandria under the same roof, and they were always arguing.

Now that Maria was involved with the Bagarozys, she thought of eventually going to Italy, mentioning that her teacher Elvira de Hidalgo had warned her about coming to America, that her real future lay in Italy, and that everything would follow naturally. But Maria wanted her mother, her good luck, with her before she made any definite plans. Her godfather, Dr. Lantzounis, had recently visited Litza in Athens and was now back in New York. Maria went to him, expressing how much she needed her mother with her, but that her father was typically acting like a pauper when she knew that he had money in the bank. He had refused to send her the money for the fare, and neither she nor her mother had enough. Dr. Lantzounis was a quiet, kind man. Without much ado, he loaned her $700. For him, it wasn't a loan. It was a gift.

So in late fall of '46 Litza made the trip. She had never been a good sailor, and even on the usually calm Mediterranean from Piraeus to Marseilles she was seasick. From Marseilles she traveled by train to Paris, then to the coast, and took the ferry across the English Channel. She was constantly sick. On the *Queen Elizabeth*, she was very seasick.

Litza arrived in New York City on Christmas Eve. Maria already had her father completely refurnish a room in his apartment with fairly expensive furniture. Separated all those years, and having grown apart before that, Litza was merely living there as a friend, a "sister." She wasn't in the least concerned about Alexandria and what went on in Alexandria's bedroom at night. Maria, however, would not accept it at all.

It was in the following year of '47 that Litza had a homecoming for me, and I saw the family often after that. Maria couldn't quite understand why I had stayed in the army all that time. She was convinced that I had been in prison and told me I even had a prison pallor.

I couldn't get over how big and fat she had gotten. But what I really couldn't get over was how her voice had developed. I would find myself staring whenever she practiced. Alexandria, who didn't like Maria's singing at all, would always go around making faces, holding her hands to her ears.

I thought that was a hell of a thing with all of them living under the same roof. Maria would only refer to Alexandria as her father's mistress, the idiot. She would pretend that the affair didn't bother her at all and would even joke about it. Once she told me, "Father can't resist sneaking into her bedroom every night. Sounds like a volcano erupting."

One evening, Litza was showing me the family album while George was away. I had seen many of the photos before, including many of the family and the girls as children. Litza had flipped over some pages, showing Maria and Jackie as young women in Athens, and then displayed several of Maria as an aspiring diva on stage, as well as Athens' prima donna. When Litza showed me a photo of a German officer, I was bridled a bit, having fought in the war, but I said nothing about it.

The photo was of Oskar Botman, she explained, a very nice boy. Still I said nothing. I had never heard of a frail Jerry, but to Litza he was frail. She sadly told me how he had died of his wounds and how she had only learned about it after the war. I wasn't particularly unhappy about it. I was very untruthful when

I said that he looked like a gentleman. "Oh, he was," said Litza. "Wasn't he, Maria?"

Maria was concerned with a score of Puccini's *Turandot* at the piano, accompanying herself, and vocally going through it *sotto voce*. "What?" she asked.

"Oskar. Oskar Botman. Wasn't he a gentleman?"

Maria kept on *sotto voce*.

Litza stopped at a photo of an Italian officer in profile, an impressive man in his uniform and cap. He looked as though he was ready to bark orders.

"This," Litza said, and her eyes were shining, "was our colonel, Colonel Mario Bonalti from Verona. Isn't he handsome?"

"Oh, yes," I said. He looked like he could bite somebody's head off.

"So talented."

"At what?" I asked.

"He played the piano beautifully, as well as Maria and Jackie. He loved to accompany Maria. Sometimes Jackie, too. He helped us so much during the occupation. Poor man is paralyzed now. The Germans," she explained, "when they took over the Italian bases. They captured him, putting him into a prison camp, until the Russians freed him, only we didn't know it then. He suffered, the poor man. We would love to see him again."

Maria's voice suddenly went to a full *forte*, coming down hard with chords.

Litza sadly turned the stiff page, showing a photo of several English soldiers with herself, Maria, and Jackie. Everyone was very happy in the photo, while Maria was a little forlorn and intent on her mother seated with a soldier. "This," Litza told me, "was just after the day of the liberation, a glorious day."

Maria stopped suddenly, glanced at the photo, and was sullen as she left. We heard Maria slam the door to her room.

Litza continued to show the photos, pretending nothing had happened.

Maria was even more sullen when I went to her room.

"What do you want?" she asked.

"Nothing," I said.

"Then why are you here?"

"Thought maybe we'd disturbed you. All right. I just wanted to talk to you."

Maria as Medea, one of her finest roles.

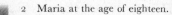
2 Maria at the age of eighteen.

3 Jackie Callas, Maria's older sister.

"What about? The Germans or the Italians? Or my mother? Hope you enjoyed the rogue's gallery."

"Why's that upset you?"

"Go figure it out."

I started away, and she said, "Listen."

I stopped, and she said, "Oh, never mind. Go look at some more of those nice pictures. They really are nice pictures."

She said nothing else, and neither did I.

One afternoon I was to meet Maria at Walgreen's Drugstore, not far from the Met. I had been waiting for some time when she came in. Her face was pinched and drawn when she took the stool beside me, and I asked her if she wanted some coffee.

"No, nothing," she said.

"What's bothering you?"

"Wasn't such a good idea to meet here," she said. "We're not far from the Met." Then she started to tell me about her Met audition, and all about the director, Edward Johnson. "I still get angry when I think about it. Oh, that pompous, snobbish, conceited ass, that Johnson. Oh, how I could have killed him. You know, I offered to do Tosca for nothing. I even offered to do Aïda, just so I could get up there, just once. He wouldn't have to pay me anything. 'Darling,' he said, that pompous, arrogant bastard, 'you're not ready for the Met.' Oh, he'll pay for that, pay and pay, even if I have to sell my soul to the Devil."

"Take it easy," I said.

"Take it easy? Oh, no. I'll never forget that. You know what the famous Met really is? It's a snooty stupid director who has to impress his board of trustees—or whatever the hell they are—with names. You just have to have a name. Then, darling, they all want you. Kiss your feet fourteen times to get you. Well, that's what I'm going to do, have them kiss my feet fourteen times and one for good measure. And they will never, *never* get me back to sing for nothing. Oh, no. It will be double."

Then she sat quietly for a long time. Finally she said, "Have you been waiting long?"

"Thought you abandoned me. Must be my fifth coffee. Lousy coffee besides. Listen, there will come a time when they'll beg you to sing at the Met."

"I certainly hope so."

"I know so. What the hell, you're better than Risë Stevens, for Christ's sake. You're miles ahead of her."

"You really think so?"

"I know it. Just get yourself a big name, then kill them bastards. So what did you audition at the Met?"

Her hand had made a grand caricatured gesture, touching her breast. *"Butterfly,"* saying it as though she was singing, as though she was Cio-Cio-San, never to see her Pinkerton again. "Some of it anyway. Wasn't bad either. Did some Mimi, too."

"And they didn't like that?"

"Why should they? Haven't got the name. That's what it is really." She didn't sound nearly as bitter or angry as before. "That can kill you. Well, goddamn it, they're not killing me."

"Oh, I believe you. Listen, if you should happen to get a good price from the Devil, let me know. Maybe we can both talk a deal."

"What? Oh." She smiled broadly. "Well, if I ever do, Stephanaki, I'm keeping it for myself, all for myself."

I didn't take her seriously. But years later I wondered about it, all right. I also wondered if the Devil actually was a short Greek with a raspy voice who sailed around in a huge white yacht. At least that was a different concept, and probably far more accurate, of what the Devil is really like.

Very often, Maria would berate George. She would say he was a lousy louse of a father who was a miser and who couldn't keep his hands to himself as far as the ladies were concerned. But Alexandria annoyed Maria the most.

One night, just after a Sunday dinner, Maria was accompanying herself at the piano and Alexandria went around holding her ears, saying that all the noise was shattering her eardrums. Maria, who was singing the *Lakmé* "Bell Song"—and there wasn't a single soprano at the Met who could have matched her trills—got up from the piano, still singing, took a heavy oval spaghetti platter that was all of two feet long and a foot across, hit her high note, and without any pause whatsoever, brought the big platter right down on Alexandria's head, shattering the dish.

We all stopped, but Maria went right on singing without a discernible interruption in her voice. Alexandria, lying on the floor, was not moving, and her hair was matted with blood. Then George shouted, "What have you done?"

"What I should have done to that pig," said Maria.

George went rushing to the kitchen. He came back with a glass of water, spilling its contents everywhere. He tried to take Alexandria's head in the crook of his arm. It rolled. He tried to get her to take some water. Her face looked bad. Litza, flinching and closing her eyes, stepped over Alexandria.

Alexandria began to moan, her head going from side to side. Water ran from her mouth. As she choked, her eyes squeezed shut, then came open. Then she saw Maria.

She let out a godawful scream and rushed to the window, shouting, "Police! Police! *Police!*" She then ran for her room, scrambled to lock her door, and still screamed for the police. George kept trying to reason with her through the door.

A police squad car pulled up in front of the building. Litza quickly picked up the slivers of the platter, and then ran to her room, yelling, "I didn't see anything! I wasn't here!"

"Well, what do we do now?" I asked Maria.

I had never seen her as nervous before. Her hands trembled, her lips quivered, but more than that, even her complexion seemed to change to a sickly pallor. It was as though, quite suddenly, a lion had been transformed into a rabbit. I couldn't believe it. I watched all this with my mouth open, firmly closing it as she answered the door at the first knock.

"Officers," she said to the two policemen, "oh, I'm so glad you've come. We locked her in her room so she wouldn't hurt anyone else."

"You the one screaming?" asked one policeman who was tall and blond.

"No, no, officer. Our housekeeper. She's a lunatic. An absolute lunatic. Butting her head against the wall like a billy goat. My God. Shouting that she wanted to die. Shouting that we were poisoning her. Shouting for the police."

"Oh, she's nuts, all right," I said.

"God," said Maria, "she's obviously a Bellevue case for your white-jacket boys."

"All right. Where is she?" asked the other.

They followed us down the long hall to Alexandria's room.

Maria knocked softly. "Alexandria?" she said. "Please open the door. No one is going to hurt you. Please, there's only someone here who wants to help you."

Alexandria let off that awful scream again.

"You see?" said Maria.

"Let us handle it," said the blond policeman. He rapped the door with the flat of his hand, hard. "Open up, lady. Police."

"Better get back," the other said.

Maria winked at me. Her face was pale, her lips and hands trembling, but she winked. I was worried. Alexandria's door was locked from the inside, although Maria had told the police she had locked the woman in. In the living room, George sat nervously on the sofa, waiting.

There was a murmur from Alexandria as her door opened. Then she was shrilly shouting hysterically in Greek, "Thank Christos! Thank Christos you came! She is crazy! She tried to murder me! Look at me!"

The blond policeman was holding her up by the arm, bringing her into the living room. A bloody towel was pressed to her head. Blood ran along her face and neck. She was still yelling that Maria tried to murder her. The same policeman asked, "You people understand what she's saying?"

A frightened Maria took two steps back, coming behind me, saying, "Good God, she's accusing me of *that*. *Me!* Did you ever hear of anything so idiotic? Why doesn't she accuse my cousin? He's bigger than I am."

"Hey, I didn't hit her," I said.

"God," said Maria, "she's deranged. Anyone can see that. She scared us nearly to death."

The blond policeman spoke to Alexandria. "Lady, you understand me? You want to make a complaint?

"She doesn't speak English," Maria said, and when the police looked at George, she told them, "He doesn't speak English either."

"Better take them to the station," said the other policeman. "Her and the injured party."

"What?" said Maria. "Are you arresting me?"

The blond policeman said, "When we get somebody to understand her, and she signs the complaint, you're going in the lockup."

"This is stupid. I explained what happened."

"Yeah, you did, but she didn't," he said. "Come on, lady. You don't want her bleeding all over your nice carpet, do you?"

Maria took her coat from the closet. "Can my cousin come along?"

"He hit her too?" asked the other.

"Steve, you'd better come with me," Maria said.

At the station house, we had to wait by the squad room while the police surgeon attended to Alexandria. They had gotten her an interpreter, and when he and some others came out, he whispered to the desk sergeant.

"May I say something?" Maria asked.

The desk sergeant, a tough Irishman, ignored her. Afterwards, he waved her over. "All right. What's your name?

"Sir, I would like to know if I'm under arrest."

"Soon as she signs the complaint."

"This really is idiotic."

"Yeah, yeah. What's your name?"

"Maria Kalogeropoulos."

"Jesus. How do you spell *that?*"

She told him. He had her repeat it a second time, and a third. All the while he shook his head, writing it down. "How old?"

She told him.

"Where do you live?"

She told him.

"Single?"

"Single."

"You do what, Maria?"

"You mean my profession?"

"Where do you work? I haven't got all night."

"I don't work. I'm an opera singer."

"Hey, Joe," he called to the cop sitting at the lower desk, "we got us an opera singer."

Joe glanced up dully from his desk and then went back to his papers.

"Got a lawyer?" the desk sergeant asked Maria. "Anybody you want to call?"

"No one."

"All right. What did you hit her with? She says a dish."

"A dish? How could a dish have done that? That's idiotic."

He waved his pencil. "Says it was a dish, and that's what I put down, a dish."

"But I've already told the two police officers what really happened."

"Yeah, yeah." The desk sergeant shook his head as he wrote. "A dish. What started it? Not that I care."

"Steve, will you please explain to the sergeant what really happened?" Her eyes were going very wide.

"You don't tell me," said the sergeant. "You tell the judge." He was still writing. "You sing a lot?"

"What?"

"You sing loud?"

"Of course."

"Sure as hell wouldn't want you living next door to me."

Just then he looked up. A detective came out from the squad room, shaking his head, no.

"All right," said the sergeant. "Get out of here."

"You mean I'm free to leave?" asked Maria.

"You want it any better? She's not signing. So do us a favor, Maria. Get out of here."

"Thank you, sergeant," she said.

Once we were outside, a timid, frightened Maria completely transformed once again. She burst out laughing, all of her big and pillowy, shaking all over.

"You were really beautiful," I said.

"I can be anything I want to be."

"Christ, I believe it."

We went along the dark street with glaring streetlights. I kept looking at her, shaking my head and smiling.

"Serves her right," she said. "She'll think twice before letting Father sneak back into her room."

"Thought you didn't care."

"Don't talk dribble," she said.

After that, Maria assaulted Alexandria at least four more times, and once or twice Maria was again taken to the station house. It was said that Alexandria would never sign the complaint because she was afraid that it would hurt Maria's father. I think it was really because she was deathly afraid of what Maria would really do.

At that time, Eddie Bagarozy was planning all sorts of things for Maria, going around as enthusiastically as a young Sol Hurok after Feodor Chaliapin. With the help of an Italian impresario named Scotto, he formed around Maria an impressive array of artists from Italy's opera houses, including Nicola Rossi-Lemini, the son-in-law of Maestro Tullio Serafin, as well as a score of artists from the Vienna State Opera. He dubbed the troupe the United States Opera Company, and with promised financial support, he hoped to have the company debut with Puccini's *Turandot* at the Chicago Opera House. Eddie also managed to get out press stories of a mysterious Greek soprano, "Marie Calas."

Rehearsals for *Turandot* were held in Eddie's small apartment overlooking the Hudson River. Maria's voice alone could make a chandelier dance on a thirty-foot ceiling. But a full chorus of fifteen additional voices was too much in a living room that could barely accommodate them all, with Eddie's dog, Baby, howling off-key right along with them.

The neighbors were going slightly insane. They called, knocked on the walls, knocked on the door, screamed at Eddie. When rehearsals went on each and every night and well into the morning the police would arrive, telling the troupe to knock off all the noise. Such is a musician's lot.

I have heard of similar things happening to musicians. I had a piano teacher, Maria Ray, a favorite of Villa-Lobos and a fine pianist, who had to endure a neighbor knocking with a two-by-four on the walls whenever she practiced, making her so nervous she couldn't play at all.

And I have had my share, too. Once I had a neighbor, a complete musical moron, who would pound, stomp, or twiddle the dials of his TV at full volume whenever I played, even if my selection was Debussy. I have even had an aspiring but lousy diva making all sorts of surreptitious complaints. Yet for years she only sang vocal exercises in triads, driving the other tenants crazy, and I was the only one who would put up with her. Only once did she grace me with her entire repertory, which wasn't very much, singing as loudly as she could, practically over my shoulder, while I blissfully played the first movement of Beethoven's "Moonlight" Sonata. You couldn't say very much for her vocal projection when I could drown her out, playing at a triple *pianissimo* yet. I could really kill her with Liszt's "Funérailles,"

Six

As luck would have it, Giovanni Zenatello, once a famed tenor and the artistic director of the annual Verona Festival, was in New York looking for a soprano for Ponchielli's *La Gioconda*. His preference was Zinka Milanov, and he was also considering Herva Nelli.

Nicola Rossi-Lemini, who remained in Manhattan, urged Maria to audition for Zenatello, while at the same time Eddie Bagarozy went after Zenatello, telling him that he had a better singer than Milanov. Zenatello didn't believe it, but he was quite willing to give Maria an audition as a possible understudy.

At Zenatello's Central Park West apartment, Louise Caselotti accompanied Maria on the piano as she sang the aria "Suicido!" Zenatello was so overwhelmed by what he heard that he excitedly took the score, turned its pages to the third act, and told Louise, "Please, please, play this." It was the duet between Gioconda and Enzo, and he happily asked Maria to sing with him.

Zenatello, who was in his seventies, sang the duet as though he were in his forties, kissing and congratulating Maria afterwards, so pleased and honored to have sung with her. She would be his Gioconda, not Milanov, not anyone else.

Eddie drew up the contracts for six performances at the Verona Festival at 40,000 lire (about $60) each. He told Maria they could forget about his commission for now, but he reminded her that they eventually would have to have a written agreement. "The money isn't much," he said, "but it's a step in the right direction. I just might have a gold mine on my hands."

There was still a problem of Maria getting the fare to the festival, and when she approached her father, he was so angry that she would be going to Italy that he wouldn't give her a penny. "Not a penny," he shouted. "Next it will be the North Pole."

Litza had no money to speak of. Still, there was Dr. Lantzounis. And once again, her godfather came through. All in all, Maria had enough money for the fare and for approximately one week to live on, ten days if she stretched it. She had to make it in Italy.

She was concerned about the Italians liking her voice. These wouldn't be the Italian troops who would be pleased with anything she did. Her voice was not a typical Italian soprano voice and it took some getting used to. If Italian opera buffs didn't like a singer, they not only threw rotten vegetables, they threw benches. The first thing Maria had to do was buy off the claques. When I asked her how she was going to accomplish all this without money, she told me she hadn't figured that one out yet. "Well," I told her, "don't get hit with a bench."

"Ha!" she said. "I'll throw it right back."

By the time I got to the gangway of the ship, a battered, converted freighter, visitors were being called ashore. The only thing that was impressive about the tub was its foghorn. Maria was standing at the railing with Louise Caselotti and Nicola Rossi-Lemini. She was smiling and waving, and I waved back, but I doubt if she saw me.

Litza scolded me a bit, asking what had happened, why I hadn't seen Maria off. I explained that I had gotten stuck in crosstown traffic.

This was the first and last time I would meet Eddie Bagarozy, and both he and Litza looked a bit put out. When I asked what was wrong, Litza told me that Maria had been in a miserable mood, pushing Eddie away, and, of all things, was jealous of Litza talking to the purser.

Maria very often was jealous of her mother, jealous of the

way men looked at her and not at Maria. I had seen it often enough. And once Maria told me that men had always been more interested in Jackie and her mother, probably because, and she was sure of it, she was "so sloppy and fat."

I would never mention her sister, Jackie, because the mere mention would upset Maria. Although I hadn't seen Jackie since she was nineteen, recent pictures of her proved her to be stunning. She had grown into quite a beautiful woman in Athens. I once told Maria that she could be a damned good-looking woman if she lost some weight. I didn't believe it, but I had said it anyway. I don't think she believed it either, although for a while before her trip she had started taking off some pounds.

But I could imagine her mother in Maria's stateroom, the purser eyeing Litza and not her daughter, and Maria getting angry, as she always would.

I learned afterwards why Maria was angry at Eddie. She wrote and told me that he had insisted she sign the agreement with him before sailing. The agreement made him her exclusive personal representative for ten years, and ensured him of ten percent of her hide, as she put it. Well, when it came to money, there was no one tighter than Maria. Money was her hedge against famine and war.

Maria wrote that her trip on the ship to Naples was awful. Her stateroom was as small as a prison cell, had mice and rats, and the food was atrocious. She ate only the potatoes and gained back most of the weight she had lost before she left. Naples, a very dirty city, was not a pleasant sight. "To think that our ancestors once occupied it," she said. "Now they wouldn't be caught dead in it." As an afterthought, she asked, "Why weren't you at the ship?"

She liked Verona far better than Naples, and whenever she wrote me from the Hotel Accademia, she would include long phrases in Italian that I would have to get translated. She wrote that rehearsals were to begin in mid-July and that the conductor would be Tullio Serafin.

It was during the rehearsal of *La Gioconda* that Maria sprained her ankle. It may have been because she was so nearsighted and was unfamiliar with the stage, or maybe she just got carried away with her role and went sprawling off her feet. But she scrambled right up again and kept on until the concluding third act before she even complained, and a doctor was called in.

Before her first performance at the huge Verona Arena, she made the mistake of putting on her glasses and peeking from behind the curtain. Seeing all the faces out there, some 20,000 faces, terrified her. She felt her throat choking up, and said, "I shook like a leaf." It was nearly impossible for me to picture Maria terrified, but apparently she was.

For her performances, she managed to hobble around with a bandaged ankle without seeming to hobble. As soon as she opened her mouth, she forgot all about her stage fright. Now, without her glasses, the audience was just a blur, although a huge blur.

It turned out she was bombarded neither with rotten vegetables nor benches. But Richard Tucker, her Enzo, got more applause than she did. I know that didn't sit too well with her. All in all, though, the audience was quite content with her performance, if nothing more, although one critic wrote that her voice was most moving and of an individual quality.

She told me that she had met this little pipsqueak of an Italian millionaire who thought he was something of a lady's man. It seemed he had a preference for divas, the chestier the better, and he claimed to be in love with her at first sight, which was perfectly ridiculous to her. "But maybe he likes them fat," she added. The whole thing to her was silly because he was at least thirty years older than she, if not more. Still he had oodles of money, was willing to take her anywhere, do everything he could, finance and help her with her career, and introduce her to only the most important people. "Now *that*," she said, "is an important consideration. Think I'll take him up on it. It can't hurt, not when he's paying for my hotel and all the food I can eat. Wouldn't you do the same, especially if you didn't know where you next meal was coming from?"

Maria may very well have been remembering Athens under the occupation and the civil war. She always seemed to make an oblique point, never a direct statement.

"The pipsqueak" turned out to be Giovanni Battista Meneghini. To her, it didn't matter that he was a lot shorter and a lot older. It didn't matter a hill of worm-eaten peas, which was another suggested reference to the occupation.

After her six performances as La Gioconda, it was difficult to keep up with her. Her career was finally beginning to go her way. She was asked to repeat her performance as La Gioconda in a town near Milan. Although she was forced to pass that up when she was about to give an audition for the director of La Scala, some absurd accounts had it that she had refused to sing there because of the contract, and another that she was too fat. The audition may not have gone as well as she liked, but she was promised she would be considered for a forthcoming production of Verdi's *The Masked Ball*.

Tullio Serafin was scheduled to conduct Wagner's *Tristan und Isolde* at the Fenice Theater in Venice. He had been so impressed with Maria's Gioconda that he sent an associate to sign her up for the part of Isolde. Maria jumped at the opportunity. But there was one problem. She didn't know Isolde. And even if she did, she doubted that she could be as Wagnerian as Kirsten Flagstad.

When she arrived in Milan the following day and told Serafin all this, he scoffed at her. She would be as good or better than Flagstad, and a month of hard study was all she needed.

She contracted with the Fenice Theater for several performances as Isolde and Turandot. Then there were no letters for a month and a half, perhaps more. When finally she did write, she told me that she had at last achieved her first real success. Now she was tucking into her letters not only Italian, but some German phrases as well.

Louise Caselotti, who was auditioning everywhere and getting nowhere, didn't like Maria's Turandot and told her she was very unhappy with it—there were none of the soaring high notes that Louise so much admired; there was a loss of freedom; Maria wavered badly; her low register was weak; and finally Louise said that Maria was on the wrong track. Maria didn't take kindly to this appraisal, and afterward she wouldn't have anything to do with Louise.

Eddie Bagarozy came to Rome to bring his wife home, although not before seeing Maria. But Maria wasn't having anything to do with him either. When he learned she was taking a plane, he found out the flight number and went to the airport to meet her. Maria took another flight to avoid him.

No matter how she justified it, one thing was clear. Maria didn't need the Bagarozys any longer.

Maria had quite a few things to say about Tullio Serafin after being holed up with him at his villa learning the role of Isolde. He would work her until she was ready to drop and then badger or exhaust her even further.

Early that summer of '48, Maria studied *Norma* with Serafin, and I could imagine how that was going. In July she sang the role of Turandot in Verona, and in August she sang as Aïda in Rome's amphitheater at the Caracalla baths. This was followed by an appendix operation, causing her to cancel an engagement in Florence. Maria wasn't very happy at this point, but neither that nor anything else was going to keep her down. From her hospital bed, she prepared for the winter season.

It was Serafin's choice to have her do a new production of Wagner's *Die Walküre*. The people of the Fenice Theater would rather have had a German import, but Serafin convinced them to allow Maria to do Wagner, because her voice knew no limitations. So most of that fall Maria studied until Serafin was convinced that she was Brünnhilde. I could imagine her *Ho-Jo-To-Ho*-ing with that classic Greek face, which no doubt she was able to transform into one of a martial Viking. Maria was prepared for the season when she arrived in Venice, but there was an unexpected turn of events.

The morning after Maria arrived at the Hotel Regina, she was awakened early by Serafin on the phone. He sounded very apprehensive and told her to come down to the salon immediately. Though annoyed at having been awakened from her sleep, she headed for the salon, wondering what in the world he wanted this early in the morning.

In the salon, she was faced by the maestro and several very worried Fenice Theater officials. They all began talking at once, asking if she knew *I Puritani* and demanding that she sing it.

She looked at them as though they had all gone crazy. "Here?" she asked.

Serafin took both her hands affectionately and explained that their leading coloratura was to have sung Elvira, but the poor child was quite ill with influenza. There was only six days till her performance, and there was no other replacement but Maria. Serafin assured the theater officials she could do it. "So as a favor to me, will you sing it? Yes, here."

"The whole thing?" she asked.

"No, no, no," he said. They would be content with an aria in order to make a decision.

She did sing for them. All the while she wondered just what time in the morning it was.

The story got around, one of those interesting fables about Maria, that she only knew the one aria and didn't have the vaguest notion of the rest of Elvira's role, neither the music nor the plot, and that she learned Bellini's entire score in six days.

The truth was that she had studied the aria with Hidalgo, lip-read the opera entirely, then worked through it on her own long before she was implored by the Fenice officials. She did put on the finishing touches as she worked with Serafin during the next five days. But what was truly remarkable was that she successfully pulled off first Brünnhilde, and then, two nights later, Elvira.

After that, she was known as a phenomenon. She could do the impossible. To live up to this claim, she sang anything and everything. For her first radio broadcast in Turin, she sang the *Liebestod* from *Tristan,* and a couple of arias from *I Puritani,* among others. Afterwards, she wrote about the Met's director, "If only Eddie Johnson could see me now. He'd be eating his heart out."

"Titta," she wrote, which was a nickname for Meneghini, was still after her to marry him. She didn't quite know what to do about it.

This had been going on for nearly two years and she had drawn flak from his family, who maintained that the family business was suffering because all his attention was being given to Maria—and besides, she was not of their world and a foreigner. They said Meneghini was just making a fool of himself and his family with all his attention for this young opera singer, this opportunist.

Maria didn't fare any better with her own family. Her

father, George, was furious that she was carrying on with a man "old enough to be her grandfather" (I couldn't see how that was possible), while Litza was almost equally adamant, writing that Maria didn't have to marry a man so much older, even though he had been a great help to her. It didn't matter how rich or influential he was, Litza wrote. Maria's future was now assured. The best thing was to remain friends with him but not marry.

It seemed that Maria's sister, Jackie, didn't have an opinion one way or another. Maria said I was the only one who agreed with her about him. All I did was to tell her to take him for all he was worth.

When Maria asked her mother to send her baptismal certificate to her as soon as possible, Litza sent it along with a letter stating that she was praying every night and every Sunday at St. Spyridon that Maria would not marry this man. But if Maria did marry him, she had to consider that if she had children, before the children were grown, they could be without a father. Maria had to think of these things.

Maria did, and she made up her mind. In the Chiesa dei Filippini in Verona, Maria and Meneghini were married. There was no one to represent his family or hers, not even friends. Then they sent off cables to their families: "We are married, and we are happy."

Years later, when Maria was interviewed and Meneghini's name came up, Maria said glowingly, "I knew he was *it* five minutes after I first met him." But she failed to account for why it took her all of two years to marry him. Or why she sailed aboard the S.S. *Argentina* the very next day after her marriage without the groom.

Seven

Maria arrived in Buenos Aires with Tullio Serafin and a group of young singers, including Mario Del Monaco, Fedora Barbieri, and Nicola Rossi-Lemini. At the Colón Theater, she wasn't always happy with her performances in *Turandot* or *Aïda*, but was almost satisfied with her performance as Norma, and thought her "Casta diva" came off well. What she was really concerned about was the pressure she was getting from her parents, and that Titta wasn't faring very well with his family either.

By then, I knew that Litza had made a complete turnabout over the marriage, saying that as long as Maria was happy with her new husband so was Litza, but adding that Maria's career came first and not her husband. Maria's father was still angry, although now that Maria was married to a millionaire, soon to make millions herself (and it was incredible that George ever doubted that for a moment), Maria could certainly afford to finance a new drugstore for him.

When the Buenos Aires 1949 season ended, Maria found that because the Peronist government was very stringent, she couldn't take her earnings out of the country. So she simply bought a collection of expensive furs, as well as shoes and pocketbooks in bright colors. Somehow she managed to send her mother $100, explaining that the banker was risking a jail sentence but was doing it because he was a fan of Maria's after seeing her in *Aïda*. Maria assured him that she would bail him out if he was arrested.

Meneghini had to wait four months for his wife, all the while furnishing their new apartment in the city, overlooking the Verona Arena. After Maria was home with him in Verona for approximately nine months, she left him a second time.

She was to have a limited two-week engagement in Mexico City, with a stopover of a few days in New York to see her parents. Meneghini hadn't planned on her going off alone, but apparently he had hit a snag of some sort. He later explained that as much as he wanted to, he couldn't accompany his wife, because of some urgent business he had to attend to.

Maria flew to New York toward the middle of May 1950 with her first Cetra recording, accompanied by the mezzo-soprano Giulietta Simionato. Only Maria's father met them at the airport. I was having a minor problem of my own and couldn't make it, nor could Litza, who was hospitalized with a painful eye infection, an acute iritis.

One of the things George did after Maria and Simionato were settled in Maria's old room was to take them to dinner at the Hotel St. Moritz. He seemed quite taken by Simionato, and no wonder, as she was a charming woman. He talked about opening up a drugstore of his own, saying it was too menial to work for someone else. He had it pretty well figured just how much he needed. Maria was annoyed when it became obvious just why her father, who wouldn't give the right time of day, had taken them for an expensive dinner. He wanted her or Meneghini to sponsor him. "What about all the money you've been saving all these years?" Maria asked. George told her, of course he'd been saving, but he didn't have nearly enough. "Well," said Maria, "that's too bad," and changed the subject, cutting him short.

Everyone sent Litza flowers, not only because she was in the hospital, but because it was Mother's Day. Everyone sent flowers, that is, but Maria. A very excitable and small woman who was a friend of Litza's berated Maria for not even sending her mother a single flower. Maria did act a little uppity. She had developed a high-toned way of speaking which wasn't like the Maria we knew at all. She was cold one moment and warm the next. But Litza didn't need any flowers from Maria. Seeing her was enough. Litza asked all sorts of questions about her career, telling her how happy she was for her.

I almost laughed when I heard that Litza thought Maria

was getting too thin, too thin to sustain her marvelous voice, when all along Litza had wanted her to lose weight. Maria hadn't lost that much, although she did look a little trimmer.

But Maria did not respond too well when Litza told her that George had no money for the hospital and that he had been furious at the idea he would have to pay both the doctor and the hospital.

"Oh, Mother," said Maria. "Do you have to be so stupid? Is that all anyone is going to talk about? Money?"

Then quite suddenly she turned it all around, sat on the bed, and cheerfully told her mother, "Don't be stupid. Of course I'll take care of it. Father never will. All I want is for you to get well. You're my good luck. You're going to Mexico with me, all expenses paid. So hurry up and get well."

Even though this had been stated rather airily, it was really the best medicine Litza could possibly have had.

When I accompanied Maria to George's apartment, she brought along a gift for me, her first Cetra recording. It was an exchange of gifts, I suppose, since I had given her a huge box of chocolates. She asked if I wanted her to autograph the recording. "Might be valuable one day," she said. "You never know."

"Why not?" I said.

She looped her huge signature over the dust cover. But it was just that, "Sincerely, Maria Meneghini Callas." There were no sentiments. Somehow, I was a little disappointed.

"The thing about recordings," she said afterward, "you suddenly hear what you really sound like. All the time I was hearing a different voice. Well, you do. A recording is like listening to a complete stranger. Don't think I like that too much. A serious singer should never make a recording, not until she has studied for at least ten years. Suppose I'll get used to it." Then she asked Simionato, "Isn't it awful when you hear yourself on a recording?"

Simionato held her nose and made a thumbs down gesture.

Then Maria said to me, "Father tells me you've taken up the piano, that you're not half bad. Play something."

"Are you kidding?" I said. That would like playing for Horowitz. "Besides, the piano is way out of tune."

Standing at the piano, she played a long, incredibly fast arpeggio without any pedal. "You're right," she said.

Then she sat down and played Rachmaninoff's Prelude in

G. She tossed off those fast martial chords at the beginning as though they were nothing, and she really had that old clunker singing when she played the middle section with its beautiful melody accompanied by tricky arpeggios. It would inspire anyone. Someday, I thought to myself, I will play it just like that. I'm still waiting for that to happen.

During those three days that Maria stayed at her father's apartment, she touched every base of emotions. She was moody, depressed, surly, or angry for no apparent reason, critical of everything, and then just as suddenly she was elated. It was obvious she had driven herself too hard, and it was really starting to show. I told her she had better start thinking about easing up after she was finished in Mexico.

"Ease up?" she said. "Ha!" Then, "You're right, of course. Better start finding time for myself. The trouble is there isn't any time."

When I asked her what she meant, she didn't explain it, although she said, "Fame is scary. It's worse than failure. There's always somebody trying to cut you to pieces."

That sounded like occupational paranoia, and when I asked her who, she said, "The lousy critics, the lousy claques."

She was insecure about everything and felt that nothing came easily to her, despite what the critics said. She explained that after every one of her performances, she really didn't know how she came off and would ask everyone what they thought. It was hell not knowing herself. It struck me as a strange paradox, that she was the only one who had been deprived of really hearing her own voice.

It was very warm the day they were to leave. All the windows were open in the living room. The tall plants were still. There was no breeze. It was stifling. Simionato was fanning herself with a newspaper, her upper lip sweating with all the packing. When she went to the refrigerator, she took out what she thought was a coke. Simionato let out a scream as soon as she drank from it and doubled up on the floor in convulsions.

Maria was hysterical, not knowing what had happened. But when she saw the bottle and took a smell, she called for an ambulance, telling them that Simionato had been poisoned. If she hadn't kept her wits about her, Simionato might very well have been dead. The coke bottle contained an insecticide.

After Simionato had been attended to at the hospital's emergency room, it occurred to her and Maria that they had a plane to catch. When I met them at the noisy arcade, both hurrying along for the boarding gate, I only had to take one look at Simionato. She looked like hell and was shaking all over. "Good Christ," I said. "What the hell happened?"

Maria, who was anxious to pass over their tickets at the boarding gate, said, "Stupid father. He keeps insecticides in his refrigerator. It almost killed her. He could have killed us all. Stupid, stupid!"

In Mexico City, the opera officials wanted the old warhorses, *Aïda*, *Il Trovatore*, and *Tosca*, to be performed. It took Maria some doing to have them allow her to sing the role of Norma.

After her first performance in *Aïda* with Nicola Moscona as Ramfis, she reminded him how he had ignored her in New York. Then she told him, "Niki, if you're so famous, why don't they ever let you sing Méphistophélès?"

She also had a run-in with Met tenor Kurt Baum, and the two wound up screaming at each other backstage. He was so angry with her that he swore to do everything he could possibly do to keep her from ever appearing at the Metropolitan.

Maria was getting $1,000 a performance, quite a step up from $6 worth of drachmas. When Litza joined her, staying in elegance at the Prince Hotel, she was accorded all the prestige and privileges given Maria. Her room, like Maria's, was constantly filled with flowers. Not even in Athens had Maria been so admired. In Mexico City, she was the queen and Litza the queen mother.

They were invited to all the parties. Litza loved it when Maria told everyone that her mother was "responsible for it all." Afterward, though, Litza began to wonder just how Maria meant that.

She was very aware of the change in Maria. There was a strange frigidity about her that disturbed Litza, and at the same time Maria was kind—she freely gave her $1,000 and took her on a shopping spree.

On a tour of all the shops, Maria, who had a fetish for pocketbooks and shoes, bought over a dozen shoes and matching handbags, picking out the brightest colors with a preference for red. Then she told her mother to buy herself a fur coat with the money she gave her, saying she deserved it after all these years.

Maria was like a Persian merchant with the store owner, criticizing everything that her mother tried on. When Litza settled on a mink (later identified as "Chinese mink," which had stiff short hairs and turned orangy over the years), Maria put the owner through hell, disgustedly inspecting the coat by stretching and pulling the fur, separating the hairs by blowing and feeling, and disagreeably stating that it wasn't worth the money. The owner sweated and then dropped his price. The coat still wasn't worth the price he was asking. He dropped the price a second time, and a third time to $500, explaining that this was well below his cost and that the only reason he wanted Litza to have it was that he considered it a great honor and privilege to serve such a distinguished artist as Maria. That seemed to make a difference with Maria. "Oh, all right," she said. "Wrap it up."

Soon afterwards, when Litza tried to kiss her, Maria pushed her away. "Don't," she said. "I'm not a child."

Simionato, who had witnessed this, angrily told Maria in her broken English, "If I was your mother, I give you good slap in you face. This is you mother, Maria."

Litza wanted to avoid difficulties, but it was becoming increasingly clear that she wasn't sure how she should act with her own daughter, or how her daughter would act with her. But as Litza had done in Athens, she would be backstage during intermissions, fanning Maria with a towel, and after each performance she went back to the hotel, rubbing Maria down with alcohol and helping her into bed. Then Litza would wash out Maria's lingerie which was blackened with makeup after her performances in *Aïda*. Litza felt she had to keep herself busier than she had in Athens, pretending that nothing had changed, but all the while knowing that something had.

One night after a performance, while she was readying Maria for bed, Maria asked Litza, "Why are you looking at me like that?" Then she said, "All right, Mother. What's it all about?"

Litza asked, "Why are you . . . well, so different?"

"I'm different?"

"Yes, really. What is it?"

Maria ignored the question altogether.

"Oh, I'm tired, Mother. I just want to go to bed."

"No, tell me. I want to know. Have I done something?"

"You really want me to tell you?"

"Yes. Whatever it is, tell me. I deserve to know that at least."

"Oh, Mother. Sometimes you're so stupid." This time she was smiling at her. "Why don't you divorce Father? You're so stupid to let that go on."

"Is *this* what's troubling you?"

"You've got plenty of grounds. Alexandria, for one. Name her as correspondent. I'd be your best witness. And you *can* get a divorce in New York for adultery. So why don't you? He's really a louse of a father."

"Maria, is this what you wanted to talk to me about? Really?"

Maria said nothing else, only that she was tired and was going to sleep.

When Maria was to leave for Spain to join Meneghini in Madrid, Litza went to the airport with her. "You'll need your ticket back to New York," Maria told her, and she bought it for her.

Maria had a fit when customs searched all her luggage, and then she had to pay the airline an additional $150 for excess weight. Listening to her, Litza felt relieved. This was her daughter as she always knew her, who always fought for her rights, whether right or wrong.

The very last thing Litza saw was Maria waving from the window of the plane. Litza couldn't shake the feeling that she had lost her.

Eight

*O*nce Maria was back in Verona, she took a long, long rest and didn't resume her career until the fall. With the pressures off her, she seemed happy, making jokes about Meneghini's family, some of whom, she satirically wrote, would have gone to the Pope or the Mafia to end her marriage.

She was very happy to be learning Rossini's comic *Il Turco in Italia*, an opera that was very different for her and seldom performed. She felt the role of Fiorilla would be great fun. She joked about the day, dreading it, that she would be an old and fat diva, with only a whisper of her voice. She would be at the piano, of course, in a ridiculous evening gown that did not hide her generous proportions, holding a long handkerchief almost to the floor, and even her speaking voice would crack. She would tell everyone who gathered for the event, "If you promise to be very quiet, I will now sing for you."

Il Turco was presented that fall of 1950. Shortly afterward she sang the role of Kundry in Wagner's *Parsifal* over a Rome radio station. She managed to learn the role of Elizabeth of Valois in Verdi's *Don Carlos* during all of this, and sang in *La Traviata* shortly after the new year. Rehearsals for *La Traviata* were filled with wrangles and brought her first quarrel with Tullio Serafin, although her performances were acclaimed. More Verdi followed, commemorating the anniversary of the composer with his *Il Trovatore*.

Then, finally, she was to sing at La Scala, where she was to perform *I Vespri Siciliani*. I was so happy for her, I wired a dozen roses for her opening night with a message, "Atta girl. Show them what real singing is." Litza wired her, "If only I could see you over the famous footlights, I would die happy."

Maria seemed to have a preference for seldom-performed works as *I Vespri*. But she went even further with Haydn's almost unknown *Orfeo ed Euridice*. Although I was a fan of Papa Haydn's piano literature, I had never heard of this opera, but then practically no one else had either.

Aside from a brief bout with jaundice, so that her two series of *Don Carlos* in Rome and Naples had to be canceled, Maria's career was going steadily upwards. She was prepared to do *Lady Macbeth* with none other than Arturo Toscanini. It was his daughter, Wally, who had made the introductions and arranged for Maria's audition with the maestro. It could very well have turned into one of this century's gold-label events once it was performed and recorded. For reasons that she would never say—only that the maestro was ailing—it never came off.

I did learn afterwards that Toscanini had a special preference for Renata Tebaldi and that he had personally endorsed her at La Scala.

By then, Maria had quite a following, a formidable claque. Her first recordings were attracting a great deal of attention, and she was then becoming well known to opera *aficionados* in the States. All during this time she was driving herself, without so much as a day off, either performing or studying, except when she came down with jaundice. And that had been like some sort of conspiracy by her body, which she would not allow.

I began to wonder if she had become like the girl in the fable who, once she started to dance, could not stop, driving herself faster and faster, knowing that once she stopped, she would die.

In the meantime, her private life was not going well at all, with either the Meneghini family or her own. She wrote, "I don't need this. But everybody is on my back, including mother."

Before Litza had taken her trip to Mexico City to join Maria, George insisted that she take out flight insurance, naming him as beneficiary. That didn't go over very well with Litza. No doubt

George would have finally had his own drugstore if Litza's plane had gone down.

When Litza told Maria about George and the business of the flight insurance, Maria said, "That's father, all right, all for himself." Another time, when Maria discussed the subject of Litza's divorcing George, she told Litza, "Mother, if ever I was married to such a man, treating me as he does you, I would take a hammer and break everything he owned with it."

After Maria left for Madrid, Litza remained for three days at the Prince Hotel, and the management still sent flowers to Litza's room. She wrote Maria about it, telling her she had been so proud, treated like the queen mother, after all those hard years in Athens and Maria's bitter disappointments in New York. And happily Litza told her that Maria's theatrical costumes were held on display in Mexico City for ten days.

But without her daughter, Litza felt oddly out of sorts, as she had when the war ended in Greece. When she returned to New York, and there was only George and that life, it really depressed her. She had only the picture of her dead Vacily in her room, a handsome, curly blond-haired boy of three, among her icons. She became very unhappy and wished only to return to Athens, hoping someday to meet her son-in-law and wondering when she could visit Maria and her husband in Verona. She sent a ring, a 500-year-old family heirloom to her son-in-law. It was a talisman that was to protect the wearer against hemorrhage. About all Meneghini did was to thank her for it. All the while Litza was complaining about her life with George—which was no life at all—saying that George would be happy if she jumped out of the window as long as she was heavily insured and he was the beneficiary.

On the other hand, George was wise enough not to ask Maria for any more financing of his drugstore, writing only that he was doing quite well, as well as could be expected, although he wouldn't tell his daughter that he was now working as a pharmacist for Riker's Island, one of the New York City prisons.

So Litza's letters expressed her unhappiness, while George's did not. He only expressed his pride in Maria. Forgetting what she told her mother in Mexico, Maria wrote saying that Litza shouldn't nag her father so much. She made no attention of providing her mother with the fare to Athens or of when Litza might visit her and Meneghini.

Late that year, George took it upon himself to provide Litza with the fare to Athens. After all, he reasoned, Jackie needed her, and Litza was anxious to see her daughter again. He was not in the least sorry when Litza left. Later, he got it around that Litza, quite suddenly and dramatically, left him. It was as though he had been betrayed.

Litza sailed on the *Hellas* of the Greek steamship line, going tourist class. But as soon as the captain learned she was the mother of the now-famous Maria Callas, he promptly changed her accommodations to a first-class cabin. It was a fine voyage, with parties and many expressions of interest in her and Maria, and she wasn't very seasick for a change.

For two years, Litza lived with Jackie at Patission 61. Other than the new interest in them because of Maria's fame, resulting in their going to several parties, things were not going well for them. Although Jackie was giving piano lessons and Litza sold silks for a manufacturer around town, their combined income never was enough.

Litza was appalled, too, that Jackie's talents were stagnating and neglected. She believed that Jackie's voice, a lyric soprano approaching dramatic, was better than Maria's in some ways, although she did not have Maria's range. I didn't believe it at the time, and it took years to learn that Litza was not exaggerating at all.

What Litza wanted was simply for Maria to help her sister, which, after all, wasn't so unreasonable. With Maria's power, Jackie could have doors opened that would have been impossible otherwise. Since Jackie had finally broken off her long engagement to Milton, nothing was holding her back from going to Italy.

Although Jackie had been writing her sister for quite a while, Maria's letters never hinted that her attitude had changed. Jackie was in for a surprise when she told Maria in a letter that she hoped to start a career for herself in Italy, but that she would need Maria's support.

The only endearment in Maria's letter of reply was the opening salutation: "Dearest Jackie." After that, she ripped into her sister, half in English and half in Greek. Maria wasn't in the least interested in what Jackie planned to do and would give her no help whatsoever. Then she ended the letter in Greek, saying, "If, as you say, you have no money, then, my dear, you had better jump in the river and drown yourself."

Jackie was so stunned that she shook. Neither she nor her mother believed that Maria could have written such a letter; they felt that she had to be joking. They soon learned she wasn't joking when they literally had their backs up against a wall, financially.

Litza had previously returned briefly to the States to sue George for nonsupport. He was ordered by the court to pay her $25 a week, which could not have supported Litza even in Greece. Once he was back in Athens, George simply ignored paying her anything, and there was no way she could go through the Greek courts without first going back to the States. In America, she had to depend on friends for support, which humiliated her.

Initially, her letters to Maria were not strident. But as Litza began to become more and more concerned about her future, with nothing to fall back on, her letters, understandably, began to take on a bitter edge. She reminded Maria of her sacrifices, that Maria owed her a great deal, and that she had not asked for the moon and neither had Jackie. They had not asked for very much at all, and it was well within Maria's power to help her sister whom she always adored. What Litza was asking for was no more than a crumb from Maria's elaborate table, which Maria could dismiss with one wave of her hand. A dutiful daughter would ease her burden. And as rich as Maria was, couldn't she spare her mother $100 a month, or even a dollar, when she was making so much money now and married to that millionaire Meneghini?

Maria's response was without any sort of salutation, noting that she had her mother's letter, that she could give her nothing, and that money was not flowers that grew in a garden. "I bark for my living. You are a young woman, and you can work. If you can't earn enough to live on, throw yourself out of the window."

Litza very nearly went out of her mind and considered doing just what Maria had suggested, jumping from the top floor of her apartment.

Afterward, Maria wrote me about it, saying how tired she was and how the whole business with her mother and Jackie had become a bore. "I never want to hear their names again," she said. "As far as I'm concerned, they are finished. They are dead."

I knew the best thing was to keep quiet about it. Still, I felt I had to say something.

I didn't particularly like myself when I wrote her saying I understood (I didn't). But I told her she had to bear in mind that if this exchange ever were to get out, it would be far more damaging than she could possibly imagine. She was asking for trouble. At this point in her career, she didn't need that sort of thing. I closed by saying that I would never mention it again, but it deserved mentioning for her own good.

I soon learned from her father that Maria was never to have anything further to do with me either. I began to wonder if Maria was touched with lunacy. That wouldn't have surprised me at all. Artistic geniuses supposedly are. There seemed to be no other explanation. I didn't buy it that she made such a complete turnabout because she was tired and overworked. It had to be more than that. Maybe she was so suicidal, so afraid of where her career was taking her, that she had to kill everyone around her.

Her father, George, assured me that in time Maria would come around, although he felt the best thing for now was to avoid mentioning me in his letters. He also said I should be very careful not to let it get back to her that he and I were still speaking. That was a hell of a thing, too. But I told him, "All right. It won't get back to her, for now."

Well, I didn't join in the battle, not then. That episode did not come about until years later, and *that* was really something, all right.

Book Three

Nine

George Callas impressed most people as quiet and unassuming. He only appeared to be that way. And he was a very frugal man. When he went to Mexico the following summer, he had his phone temporarily disconnected so he wouldn't have to pay for it.

Maria, who was to perform in Mexico City a second time, invited George to join her and Meneghini. Much as Litza had been, he was accorded to all the honors. It was the first time he had ever seen Maria perform. He thought her performances were nothing short of miraculous and said he always knew she would aspire to such greatness. I am sure he told all this to the inmates at Riker's Island as well. And I'm sure they were all very interested.

This was the same George who thought Maria's music lessons were a complete waste of time and, of course, money. It didn't take much imagination to know what would have happened if Maria had actually been under his inspiring hand. She would have ended up, as he wanted her, married with a parcel of kids. Naturally, she could have been married to a Greek who traditionally strayed, or who gambled every night at the local *cafenio*, while she, of course, stayed home, a dutiful wife, cooking and minding the kids. But she would have always wondered exactly what it was that she missed out on.

Or she might have become a dentist. This was one of the things she aspired to be as a child, and she was very serious. I

Litza Callas, Maria's mother (centre), with her two daughters:
Jackie (left) and Maria (right).

5 Myself with my daughter Helena and my wife Hildegard. My painting of Maria as Medea is behind me on the left.
(Photo: Franey Fabry)

All the photographs are from the author's collection.

don't know where she got that idea; and I don't think she knew either, but that was what she wanted to be, a dentist, of all things. So this is how she may have ended up, a dentist, married to a Greek, or both. If her mother had not taken her to Athens to begin with, it was conceivable that this is what could have happened. So this was a big plus for Litza.

For some perverse reason, Maria was now siding with her father. It only added gasoline to the fire when Maria invited him to join her in Mexico City. It was too much for Litza. Until then, not everyone of the immediate family knew about Maria's brutal letters to Litza and Jackie, but Litza was now so outraged, she wanted to throw the letters into the public domain. The dispute was only beginning.

Another of Maria's disputes was with Renata Tebaldi, though she and Maria had initially been friends. Tebaldi was, of course, an extremely fine soprano. But Maria did not retain friendships very long with someone she no longer needed, or with anyone who was part of the competition. The argument began over nothing at all, some silly thing that had to do with how many encores Tebaldi gave at a benefit concert in Rio de Janeiro.

Maria sang "Sempre Libera" from La Traviata, which was all she was scheduled for, while Tebaldi sang her "Ave Maria," and then two encores. The whole thing blew up over dinner a few nights later when Maria accused Tebaldi of trying to upstage her and of pathetically trying to make up, at Maria's expense, for a lousy La Traviata at La Scala the season before.

Soon afterwards, things began to happen to Maria. In Rio, after the first night she sang Tosca, the director told her he was letting her go because of poor audience response. This was humiliating for Maria. She sensed a conspiracy between Tebaldi and the director. Maria told him he still had to pay her for another Tosca and two performances of La Traviata. They had a contract. Stuck with that, the director said he would allow her to finish out her two performances of La Traviata, but he added, "Chances are that no one will want to see you."

Both performances of La Traviata were sold out. Any other director would have been elated, but not this one. He later told Maria, "I shouldn't even pay you, considering the kind of success you've had."

Maria, who had had just about enough of him, grabbed a bust of Puccini from his desk, and more than likely, *à la* Maria, as she had with Alexandria, she was about to crown him with it. But Maria was stopped just in time by Meneghini. Meneghini really had a tough time pulling her away, and at one point she nearly flew at him.

As it turned out, Maria's replacement in *Tosca* was Tebaldi. Now Maria was sure that Tebaldi and the director were part of the conspiracy to humiliate her as best they could. And they did succeed in humiliating her.

Soon afterward, Maria was to experience the Tebaldi claque at La Scala, when she was heaped with thrown vegetables, hooted, hissed, and whistled at on stage. The Callas claque retaliated equally. At times, it seemed that being a diva ran nearly the same risks as a bullfighter of being gored.

Maria was becoming *la prima donna assoluta*. I couldn't help but be proud as hell and at the same time fell like royally kicking her tail. She needed it. God, did she ever. But she was totally out of range. Anyway she might have proved too formidable an adversary. But that was what we had become, adversaries. I didn't like that at all.

Sometimes George would go on and on about Maria. His living room was becoming a gallery, containing mostly professional photos of her, many of them autographed. He was getting all of her recordings either passed on to him by Maria or the people at Angel Records. I thought it damned curious, if not downright funny, that he had become an opera buff so late in life without so much as playing any of her recordings.

Of course, I heard all about Maria, whether I wanted to or not: when her season at La Scala "electrified her audiences," or when she made her debuts at Covent Garden the season before, singing Norma, and left the usually reserved British "gasping."

I loved to put him on. "Norma," I once said to him, "isn't that where she's the rival of the Druid priestess?"

I got a kind of blank look.

"Oh, I know," I said. "Norma is really Adalgisa suffering from amnesia. Isn't that it, or do I have the wrong opera altogether?"

He changed the subject, talking about a totally different opera. At least he was beginning to love opera, so he couldn't be all bad, even if he didn't know what he was talking about half the time. But he was learning. At least that was something.

I wouldn't always get those glowing infighting accounts from him as I had from Maria. But it was from George that I learned when Maria first contracted with La Scala. The Metropolitan's new general manager, Rudolf Bing, had wished to sign up Maria and Meneghini had discussions with him, finally telling Bing that Maria would not sing at the Metropolitan as long as he ran it.

George was a little baffled about that, but I wasn't baffled at all. Maria was finally beginning to pay the Met back. She probably didn't even see Bing, and had Meneghini act as her functionary, making all sorts of excessive demands on the Metropolitan for her fee. No doubt she wanted Bing to include the bronze bust of Caruso in the Met's lobby.

Within a year and a half, Maria managed to lose over sixty pounds. I didn't know whether or not this was a result of the strain she was under, but whatever the reason, judging by her photos, she was transformed, quite surprisingly, into a trim, stunning, and very chic woman. Even her hair coloring had changed. It was the same reddish coloring as her mother's.

She drove an Alfa Romeo that Meneghini had given her. She wasn't about to drive around in any old Cadillac. And she had accumulated quite an entourage wherever she went, including the dress designer Madame Biki, who was one of Puccini's granddaughters.

In late 1954, Maria came back to the States, ignoring the Met completely, which I am sure she did with great pleasure, to sing at the Lyric Theater in Chicago.

A Milan agent for the Lyric Theater had first approached her in January. Apparently, for reasons I could well understand, she was not as tough in her demands as she had been with the Met, agreeing to open in Chicago in the beginning of November.

A month later, Carol Fox, who was one of the Lyric Theater's impresarios, finalized the contract. I am quite sure Maria must have noted that she would have made her American debut in Chicago years earlier, if only the United States Opera Company had not gone broke—but that was not Chicago's fault, only its misfortune.

Knowing Maria, she had to say that.

The contract called for six performances for a total of $12,000, and included first-class travel and expenses both ways for herself and her husband.

Maria's father, too, was to join her in Chicago. Before he left for Chicago late that fall, he once again had his phone temporarily disconnected.

After twenty years of dismal failures, Chicago was back to its operatic glory. Maria's première in *Norma* saw to that. But Eddie Bagarozy was figuratively waiting in the wings.

On November 4, a Chicago attorney representing Eddie brought suit against Maria. In effect, the suit cited her 1947 written agreement with Eddie, making him her sole representative, and asserted that Maria had agreed to pay ten percent of any and all gross earnings, whether it was in opera, concerts, radio, recordings, or television, and that said fees were to become due and payable upon receipt of monies received by her. Eddie Bagarozy, the suit went on, had agreed to use his best efforts to further and promote her career and pointed out that he had done just that, claiming he had spent $85,000 on Maria's behalf. No doubt he was referring to the expenses involved in forming the now-defunct United States Opera Company, which had been built around Maria.

The contract seemed ironclad. The suit further cited that Maria wrongfully attempted to sever the contract. The amount named in the suit was for $300,000, with attachments filed on Angel Records.

Maria denied the charges, claiming that Bagarozy's contract had been obtained under duress and that he had done absolutely nothing to promote her career, a statement which wasn't altogether true. Her career may not have gone anywhere if he hadn't gotten after Zenatello, and as a result Maria signed for *La Gioconda* in Verona.

The court ordered a deposition hearing for November 8. Maria didn't even appear. She had retained a Chicago law firm to

epresent her. It was the start of three years of legal maneuver-
ngs in the States and abroad.

Once back in Italy, Maria was not all that anxious to return
o Chicago, for obvious reasons. For Chicago, it was a must.
Maria did not want to talk business, but Lawrence V. Kelly, the
other impresario for the Lyric Theater, was very dogged. In
Milan, they would often meet at the Biffi Scala, a very elaborate
restaurant. Kelly was quite willing to discuss any and all terms,
including the incorporation of some very unusual clauses in her
contract.

The Lyric Theater would agree to accept responsibility in
protecting Maria and Meneghini against any legal harassment
and/or proceedings during the season. Only after that was incorporated into the contract, and Meneghini's attorneys went over
it, did Maria agree to sign it. Eddie Bagarozy would be left talking
to the wind. His attorneys would never even get close to her.

As was expected, her second Chicago season was another
success. Bjoerling, a tenor I have always admired and one of my
favorites, thought Maria's Leonore in *Il Trovatore* was perfection
and claimed that there had never been a better one than hers.

The same afternoon *Il Trovatore* was repeated, both Maria
and Rudolf Bing came to terms—Maria's terms. It was so embar-
rassing that Bing would not tell what the terms were.

When Bing took over as the general manager of the Met in
1950, he was against the star system, with its emphasis on the
ensemble. The star system had too many pitfalls. But Maria Callas, troublesome and difficult, was box office.

The actual agreement, which was termed "momentous,"
was signed at a dinner table. Bing gave Maria a kiss to seal the
agreement. The photographers had him repeat it several times to
get it just right. I wondered if it was all of fourteen times, and
one for good measure.

I had heard Maria punitively kept him waiting in the wings
for hours. Over at her hotel, she would ask her maid if he was
still waiting, and when she was told that he was, Maria said,
"Good. Let him wait." When finally she consented to see him,
she was overly charming. But when he went into what he could

actually pay her $1,000 per performance, which was a long-standing policy limit of the Metropolitan, she told him, "Well, you'd better think again. I'm not signing with the Met for that amount." And she didn't care if that was more than Caruso ever got at the Met. She wasn't Caruso. She was Callas.

When she was asked what amount she had in mind, she said simply, "Double." Bing assured her he would get back to her. Later, when she was asked why she didn't come to terms with the Met, she said, "The Met is not my father."

Bing finally did get back to her, signing her for the '56 season, but only after Maria put the poor man through hell. She paid the Met back, all right. And I am sure she had some very nice things to say about Edward Johnson in the process.

When a reporter wanted to know what amount she had settled on, she replied that no fee was high enough to sing *Norma*. What she really meant was Callas' *Norma*, especially at the Met.

For her final performance of *Madama Butterfly* at the Lyric, the applause was deafening. Her audience would not let her go. She was called back again and again. Finally, she gave her last bow, as only she could bow and waved her good-bye. Waiting for her were reporters and photographers, and a process server.

Process servers are not well-known for sensitivity or consideration in their manner and approach, and it cannot be said that they handle deadbeats and divas differently. They are treated alike. Since the law requires that the subject be physically handed a summons, and duly noted, the process server did so by shoving the summons into Maria's kimono since she would not voluntarily accept it.

Cio-Cio-San was immediately transformed. The fury of hell might be too mild a metaphor for her rage. A flashing camera caught that for all time, her mouth and face distorted, displaying a fury that excelled Medea's, and everything about her flying, pointing her finger and shrieking at the back of the process server.

Maria was screaming at all the reporters and photographers, "Get out! Get out!" and appeared ready to throw something at all of them. They scrambled out, some grinning, some not. Maria was screaming at everyone in sight, particularly the theater's two impresarios: "How could you let this happen? How could you do this to me?"

The two young impresarios were stunned. Meneghini was outraged, trying to console Maria, but she only shrugged him off and wouldn't allow him to touch her: "Chicago will be sorry for this," she screamed.

It turned out that Eddie Bagarozy's representatives had been very enterprising, infiltrating the very core of the Lyric Theater. It was merely a question of presenting the summons at exactly the right moment, and the right moment was after her last performance, when everyone would be very lax backstage. A simple matter, really.

The Associated Press got quite a bit of mileage out of that one photograph. Every major newspaper in the States picked it up. She was pictured as everything from a temperamental demon to a poor neglected child of the slums. Several newspapers had it that she was Brooklyn's own—that she was born there—while others had it that she was a product of New York's Hell's Kitchen.

The day after she was served the summons, she flew back to Italy, swearing never to set foot in Chicago again.

Ten

Even before Chicago, hordes of reporters would follow Maria on her daily constitutional down Via Monte Napoleone in Milan. Everything about her was news. She was *"La Callas, La Divina, Voce di Angelo"* and one German magazine, I believe it was *Stern*, had the headline, *"Engel oder Teufel* [Angel or Devil]?" Whatever she did, even posing with her toy poodle or Meneghini, was news. Her extravagance was news, and her chic bearing, which probably had every fat woman in Italy envious.

When Meneghini acquired the four-story townhouse—it was more like a palazzo—on Via Michelangelo Buonarroti, it was news. Its sumptuous exterior as well as its interiors, with red marble and Renaissance paintings, antiques, and luxurious furnishings, were thoroughly photographed.

After Chicago, then, it was not surprising that Maria's photo as the frenzied Cio-Cio-San made every Italian newspaper and magazine. Now there was another headline: THE SPAGHETTI WAR.

The Rome firm of Pastificio Pantanella, makers of spaghetti, published the claim that Maria's spectacular weight loss had come about due to a steady diet of Pantanella spaghetti. An affidavit by a Dr. Cazzarolli was incorporated in the advertisement, giving medical support.

As soon as Maria returned from Chicago, she learned of this claim. She was outraged, first wiring the company, then filing a lawsuit. The "spaghetti war" was being publicized almost daily with the sort of coverage for which any public-relations firm would have given its eye teeth. The litigation lingered on for years, until a Rome court awarded Maria damages. The decision was upheld by an appeals court.

No diva in the history of grand opera had been given coverage that so rarely had anything to do with opera. Of course, when it did, it rarely had anything to do with her performances. You could only find that tucked away on the music page.

All that massive coverage was to follow her when she landed at New York's Idlewild Airport toward the middle of October 1956. And quite a lot more was waiting for her.

To tie in with her arrival, Eddie Bagarozy lost no time in filing his suit in New York's Supreme Court, with attachments served on the Metropolitan Opera Company and Angel Records. For some reason, probably on the advice of counsel, Maria agreed to accept a summons at her hotel suite two days after her arrival.

Maria made a statement: "I'm fully confident in American justice. I do not care about attempts to frighten me through writs of attachments and other means. I am simply waiting the final ruling of an American judge who will say the last word in this boring affair."

But Maria was outraged, fuming and cursing, carrying on about Eddie Bagarozy, that he was trying to stab her in the back, to ruin it all for her, that he was greedy, and on and on she went. But that wasn't all that was to happen.

Just before the Met's season began, every newsstand displayed a *Time* magazine portrait of Maria. What was of particular interest was the four-page story about her, which hardly could have given a complete account, but it was quite enough. As her father told me, "It was absolutely devastating."

Maria was pictured as a diva more widely hated by her colleagues and more widely acclaimed by her public than any other living singer, which was quite true. There were some thoughtful facts of her musical abilities, the dramatic qualities of her voice.

But she was also depicted as ruthless. Her backstage feuds were exposed, and the tenor Giuseppe di Stefano was quoted as saying, "I'm never going to sing opera with her again, and that's final." Tebaldi was described as Maria's first victim, and the article implied that Maria had said, "She's got no backbone. She's not like Callas." A nameless source stated, "The day will come when Maria will sing by herself." There was also a report of the feud between Maria and Maestro Tullio Serafin, and that Serafin was finding other singers mysteriously unable to sing under him.

Then the *coup de grâce*—Litza.

Evangelia Callas, as Litza was generally known, had been interviewed by *Time*'s reporters in Athens and for the first time had released excerpts of Maria's last letter—with some minor variations which seemed to include Jackie's letter as well. Maria was quoted, "Don't come to us with your trouble. I had to work for my money, and you are young enough to work, too. If you can't make money to live on, you can jump out of the window or drown yourself."

Well, there it was, out in the open, at the worst possible time. George didn't have to tell me how Maria had reacted. The article's timing could not have been better.

The press coverage was bitter toward Maria. Now they had something far better to work with than petty squabbles between Maria and her colleagues, which amounted to no more than a case of spoiled children arguing over nothing. Now the press had Maria living in the lap of luxury, but allowing her mother to starve.

When reporters tried to interview her about her cruel letter to her mother, she wouldn't discuss anything with them, only say, "This had to be a crackpot who dreamed that up." Privately, she was denying it to all her friends, who were many and the very elite. They saw her only as a victim of vicious gossip, the sort that always plagued Maria, and this seemed to be a new low. Anyone who knew Maria—and they all presumed that they did— believed that Maria was totally incapable of such a thing. Still, Maria knew the truth.

When Maria appeared for her first Met rehearsal, I could just imagine her making an entrance in her typical grand manner, a sweeping entrance, with her yapping poodle in tow and Meneghini dutifully following a few steps behind. Maria would be telling herself that she had finally made it, the hard way.

Reportedly, she had no stage jitters whatsoever and went

over every foot of the stage. She scoffed at some of the shabby scenery, which wasn't at all like the splendor at La Scala, and considered it pretty lousy when this was supposed to be *the* Metropolitan. This, though, she stated privately. And this was before the *Time* magazine article, and the ensuing blasts by the press.

Afterward, it was a different matter. The devastation that George had pointed out was quite apparent. During her dress rehearsal of *Norma*, Maria said she had a bad cold that she was fighting off and she had a bad throat. It may simply have been psychosomatic, and probably was, recalling how Maria expressed stage fright and how her throat seemed to choke up on her, aside from her "shaking like a leaf."

In her dressing room, she had the jitters so badly that she nearly vomited. Marlene Dietrich brought her a thermos of hot broth, and I could imagine Dietrich saying in that famous deep-throated voice of hers, "Darling, here drink this, please. You will feel much, much better." And Maria, who might not have been thinking of her performance at all, but the biting press, might have said, "What are they trying to do to me? Kill me?"

For the première, the Met had to turn away over $50,000 in business, the first time in its history that anything like this had happened. Orchestra seats went for $35, and standing room was no bargain either. Ticket scalpers were getting as much as $125 a seat—sometimes even more—and it didn't seem to matter where the seats were located.

I tried to get tickets. It was impossible. With blankets in hand, people were already standing in a line that went around the block. Even Maria's father couldn't get a ticket for me. At least he said he couldn't, but he thought he might be able to do something after the première, as long as Maria didn't know anything about it.

An enterprising friend of mine, a Broadway bookie who hung out across from Lindy's and who was mob-connected, said he would have no trouble getting me tickets, but added, "You'll have to come up with some good bread." Then he asked, "But why do you want to see that dizzy screwball? You that much of an opera nut?" In keeping with the conversation, I told him, "Yeah."

"No kidding? That's very nice." Then he went on how he used to like Nelson Eddy and Jeanette MacDonald. I only wanted to know if he could get the tickets.

"You don't hear so good," he said. "I told you I could, didn't I? But I don't know what you're so worked up about seeing that crazy broad, not when she shits all over her poor mother."

Well, there it was, the popular opinion. Charming to hear it from a bookie, mob-connected besides, with strong feelings about motherhood. Christ. I never told him I was Maria's cousin. I might never have gotten the tickets if I had. And he was doing me a big favor, or so he said. The scalper only wanted double what he paid for it, only because I was such a good friend of the bookie. The scalper, the bookie said, could have gotten a lot more, a whole lot more.

It seems that friendships are very important sometimes, even in the worst of circles.

Other than the usual sparkling bejeweled asses of the Golden Horseshoe on opening night, and all the crowds, what I really expected to see were pickets outside, denouncing Maria, much as there had been for Walter Gieseking when he gave his first recital at Carnegie years after the war, and a policeman was stationed at every door. But it wasn't like that at all. There were only the usual police to contain the crowds.

My seat was atrocious. I sat behind a pole in the gallery. Still it was a seat. The lights dimmed, and the curtain rose. Finally, Maria stepped out on the stage. The applause was polite but surprisingly cool. It was nothing compared to what Barbieri and Del Monaco received, practically a standing ovation. That and the bad press didn't help her "Casta diva" at all. She barely brought it off. You could sense her fighting to keep the aria from becoming a complete disaster.

During intermission, Zinka Milanov, who merely sauntered down the aisle, got a greater ovation than Maria. I'm sure Maria wouldn't have liked that at all if she had known about it. Then, too, the standees, seemingly more Tebaldi fans, were spoiling for trouble, hoping that Maria would fall flat on her face. That was most of the conversation during intermission. "Callas was an overrated nothing."

It was quite a different matter with her second act. Her bad throat—imagined or otherwise—faded. She was magnificent. You could sense the audience reacting to her. She must have sensed it, too. She sang even better.

When the final curtain came down, she took over a dozen curtain calls, and I have yet to see anyone who could bow more graciously. It was an art form in itself. It was worth the price of admission alone.

Before any of this, I had written Litza that it was too bad she wasn't in town. If she had been, it might have made quite an impression if she stood outside the Met wearing an old shawl, something from the Salvation Army, and sold violets, and, of course, announced who she was. Now that would have gotten a reaction from Maria.

But after seeing Maria in *Norma*, I didn't like that idea at all. I had applauded as frenzied as anyone else, perhaps even more. Like most, I suppose, I separated her from her art. I was more proud of her than I had ever been. But I made no attempt to see her after the performance. It would not only have been impossible. Maria, quite easily, might have had me arrested.

An Angel Ball was given in her honor at the Ambassador Hotel, attended by the Ambassador of Greece; Rudolf Bing and his Met entourage; Cleva, who had conducted; as well as Gladys Swarthout, Giovanni Martinelli, and Marlene Dietrich, who had blisters on her hands from applauding so much.

I wondered whether or not Maria ever brought up to Martinelli the time she auditioned for him after the war and he found breaks between the registers of her voice. I am quite sure Maria felt compelled to ask him at the ball, "Well, Giovanni, was I at least acceptable this time?"

The reviews were quite mixed. The worst of them were by Howard Taubman of *The New York Times* and Paul Henry Lang of the *Herald Tribune*. Taubman thought Maria's was a puzzling voice that occasionally gave the impression of having been formed out of sheer willpower rather than natural endowments. He was only half right. Lang, who I cannot recall ever having given Maria a good review, said some good things but thought that she had vocal limitations and a veiled quality to her middle register.

There was even a full middle-page spread in the *New York*

Daily News. But that had more to do with the Golden Horseshoe during intermission. One woman, regally gowned and overweight, posed with her feet up on a table, while a white-haired man, in white tie, attempted to drink champagne out of a woman's slipper that was open at the toe and heel.

Eleven

❧

The *Time* magazine article became another issue of controversy. Renata Tebaldi took exception to Maria's assumed reference to her lacking a backbone. In a letter to the *Time*'s editors, Tebaldi wrote, "I am truly astonished at the statements made by my colleague Signora Maria Meneghini Callas regarding me. The signora admits to being a woman of character and says that I have no backbone. I reply: I have one great thing that she has not—a heart.

"That I actually trembled when I knew she was present at a performance of mine is utterly ridiculous. It was not Signora Callas who caused me to stay away from La Scala [obviously referring to Maria's fourth season there when Tebaldi was no longer with the theater]; I sang there before she did, and consider myself a *Creatura della Scala*. I stayed away of my own free will because an atmosphere not at all pleasant had been created there. . . .'"

Tebaldi, who was in Chicago, wasn't to begin her Met engagement until after Maria's had finished. It was just as well, as there might very well have been riots. The feud, though, was promoting record box office for both of them as well as increasing phonograph sales.

Tebaldi had a very powerful ally. When Maria did *Tosca* with George London, Elsa Maxwell, who was the society columnist for the *New York Journal-American*, and who was just as obnoxious about society and the arts as Howard Cosell can be about sports, wrote that Maria was the "devious diva" and that she did not like her performance in the first act, or the way she sang "Vissi d'arte," or her dramatic exit at the end of the second act. Maxwell even found a bit of jealousy in the way Tosca (Callas) had sent Scarpia (London) to his doom.

This, of course, was ridiculous. *Tosca* was one of the finest things that Maria ever did, even though she was bored to death with it. Any musical moron would have seen the merit of her performance when a portion of the second act was televised nationally over TV's "Ed Sullivan Show" late that November 1956.

Maxwell was motivated, no doubt, by her adoration for Tebaldi. What may have motivated the "bit of jealousy" was what went on during the broadcast rehearsal.

George London couldn't find his mark and fell too close to the desk, and Maria couldn't pass to cross the stage. The way London told it, Maria stopped in her tracks, and then told the director, "There are too many legs around here," and they all had a good laugh.

Dorothy Kilgallen's column in the *New York Journal-American* had it: "Maria Callas caused her vis-à-vis, George London, to flip his talented lid. The tempestuous prima donna at one point stopped in the middle of an aria to accuse London of pushing a chair out of line, and in the death scene she stopped the music to cry out, 'There's too much feet in my way.' "

The latter made for a better story, at least for the press. There was nothing very exciting about missing the mark and having a good laugh.

Before George London ever worked with her, he admitted that he had quite a few qualms, since so much had been printed about Maria, and that he was prepared for anything.

He was pleasantly surprised to find her a trouper, a fanatical worker, a stickler for detail, and very pleasant. Whether London was being kind to her, I don't know. But it's quite possible this was the way he found her to be. She could turn on the charm at times, and she knew the value of it. She shared the philosophy that if you can't beat them, join them. And that's exactly what she did with Elsa Maxwell, charming the hell out of her.

By then, Maria had sung at the Met, in Philadelphia, and at a function at the Italian Embassy in Washington, D.C., that was attended by all sorts of dignitaries, including Sherman Adams, President Eisenhower's adviser. At a dinner dance given at the Waldorf-Astoria in New York for the American Hellenic Warfare Fund, Maria was introduced to Elsa Maxwell by Spyros Skouras, who then headed Twentieth Century-Fox.

Maria took one look at Maxwell, as round as a huge beachball, as ugly as an English bulldog and, holding her breath, Maria emitted all her charm. Maxwell imagined herself to be the last person on earth that Maria would wish to meet. Maria, probably lying through her lovely teeth, said, "On the contrary, you are the first one I wish to meet because, aside from your opinion of my voice, I esteem you as a lady of honesty who is devoted to tell the truth."

Elsa Maxwell was later to say, "When I looked into her amazing eyes, which are brilliant, beautiful and hypnotic, I realized she is an extraordinary person."

Maria, it seemed, had completely neutralized a powerful adversary. But that wasn't all Maria was after. Maxwell knew only the most influential, wealthiest people in the world, was much in demand for her services for these all-important introductions and, according to George and other sources, Maxwell charged quite a fee. Not only was Maxwell to prove very useful in this regard, but she also served as Maria's spokesperson, fending off serious attacks against Maria.

Late that December, at New York's Supreme Court, Maria's attorney argued that Eddie Bagarozy's suit was nothing but a scheme to systematically harass Maria. The purpose of the scheme, he said, was to induce Maria to pay some wholly unjustified tribute rather than incur the substantial expenses of multiple litigation. He pointed out that a similar suit had been brought against Nicola Rossi-Lemini, and that it had been settled with a payment of $4,000. The amount was quite a contrast to the claim against Maria for $300,000.

But all this was countered very effectively by Eddie's attorney, and the case was continued. Maria wanted to end it right there and then and told the court that Bagarozy had done nothing to further her career and therefore had failed to live up to *his* end of the contractual agreement. The only one who owned her as a manager was her husband.

She returned to Italy, and did her personal story for *Oggi*, which ran in five installments. Knowing Maria, you not only could have put holes through it, but cannon shot. She ended the article by saying that she would soon return to La Scala to sing *La Sonnambula*, *Anna Bolena*, and *Iphigénie en Tauride*. Then she made the curious statement that she knew her enemies were ready for her, but that she would fight to the best of her ability, and that she would not disappoint the public who loved her, and whose esteem and admiration she was determined to keep.

After a few weeks, following the 1957 New Year, she was back in Chicago for another court appearance. While there, she accepted an engagement for a benefit concert to be given for the Hungarian Relief Fund. A few days later, she was back in New York, attending a regal costume ball annually given by the Hospitalized Veterans Service. Maria came costumed as the ancient Egyptian Empress Hatshepshut. Elsa Maxwell, no doubt for some subconscious need, came as Catherine the Great.

Maxwell later wrote about the ball in her column, and added, "It seems we are going to be friends." Maxwell was also planning a fancy dress ball in Maria's honor for the coming season of Venice's high society.

Maria was back in Chicago in the middle of January. She gave a press interview, and nearly nearly sounded as though she was running for public office when she said she had returned with no bitterness in her heart, and only had affection and gratitude for the city's devoted public. But lurking behind all that was her previous statement that she would never sing again for the same management that had betrayed her. The door was opened for reporters to ask pointedly about her angry departure from Chicago, after being hit with a summons. Maria first sighed, then smiled, and finally, thought it all out for a moment. Then she said, "Sometimes I do get angry. Temperament on the stage benefits the theater. I am otherwise a calm person. Am I not?"

Aside from her friends, I hardly think there was anyone who would agree with her.

In April, Maria had performed the unfamiliar *Anna Bolena* by Donizetti. Her performances in Milan, as had come to be expected, were sold out. Elsa Maxwell was invited to hear her at Maria's invitation. When the two met at the airport and embraced, the headline that followed the photo was, "Behold, the two tigers." Maxwell countered with an angry retort in her column about the evil web of invective that had been woven around Maria Callas.

When La Scala's season was drawing to a close, Maria was to perform Gluck's *Iphigénie en Tauride*. Elsa Maxwell flew in from Paris for the dress rehearsal and followed with an entire column on Callas. Maxwell vented her anger, "Someone somewhere is spreading poison about one of the most touching individuals I have ever known. I am going to track them down, wherever they may be. Nothing can destroy the supreme art of Maria Callas."

Before leaving for Paris, Maxwell promised to repay Maria's hospitality. So when Maria stopped off for three days to see Maxwell in Paris, it became quite a round robin of society parties, tea with the Windsors, cocktails with the Baroness Rothschild, attending the races with Prince Aly Khan, and visiting with all sorts of royalty. Maria, it seemed, reigned over all of them.

In late July of '57, following lengthy negotiations, Maria agreed to give two concerts in Athens, after an absence of over eleven years. The agreement with the Athens Music Festival was that she was to be paid expenses—both for herself and Meneghini—and 270,000 drachmas, or $9,000, which was considerably more than what she had received for all the combined years she sang in Athens.

The authorities of the music festival defended the huge fee, saying that she had once been the Kalogeropoulos girl, their own, and was now the world's leading prima donna who commanded $10,000 and more per performance. To others, she was a U.S. import who would take money out of the country. From this started a serious controversy, so serious that it threatened the overthrow of the government.

The exorbitant amount was the first thing hit on by the opposition party. The country was poor, and postwar reconstruction was arduously difficult. Then creeping into that was the widely publicized break between Maria and her mother. Then there was all that controversy which still persisted about whether she was a collaborationist during the war. The Athens press gave it quite a going over.

This created a crisis for the government, with the situation worsening daily. The government had to do an incredible amount of lobbying with the press. The Athens press would not be dissuaded. Church, country, and family were paramount. Fame did not matter as much as loyalty and decency. What Maria had done, as well as viciously discarding her mother, was despicable.

What was incredible was that it was suggested, and it got around as such, that the government, to avoid any head-on confrontation between Litza and Maria, persuaded Litza and Jackie to leave the country—in the interests of national security. And, supposedly, Litza had said that she would rather be dead than be in Athens when Maria arrived with Meneghini. No doubt, if this had been true, the press would have eagerly jumped on it and made the situation worse.

The truth was that Litza was back in New York, still trying unsuccessfully to collect the mere $25 per week from George that he had been ordered to pay by the court years earlier. Jackie was in Athens, quietly watching it all happen without even receiving an official invitation to attend the concert, and she remained unavailable for comments.

This, though, was the appalling scenario that greeted Maria's arrival at her suite at the Hotel de la Grande Bretagne, not far from where she sought safety during the civil war. What was interesting was that her wealthy olive-oil relatives, who were so disinterested in her career during those very hard war years, and even before, now sent huge bouquets to her suite, and later to the theater, even suggesting that they had a great deal to do with her career in those early days.

With all that was going on, Maria, who remained in her suite at the Grande Bretagne, wanted to run for the hills. She felt victimized—her own people were doing this to her. Then she received word that King Paul and Queen Frederika would not be present at her concert, obviously removing themselves from the explosive political situation. Maria flew into a rage, ordered her bags packed and had Meneghini call the airport to make reservations on the first plane out.

Jittery authorities of the Athens Music Festival stopped her on her way to the airport, promising that the prime minister and members of his cabinet would be at her concert, if only she would sing. Then Meneghini stated that Maria had decided to cancel her first concert because of her rundown, exhausted condition, which had been made worse by the sudden change to Athens' hot, dry weather.

I don't think it was anyone's persuasive argument that got

Maria to perform that night. It must have been her own backbone when she stepped out on the familiar amphitheater of Herodes Atticus, where she first sang in Beethoven's *Fidelio*. It had to take a great deal of courage when she was hooted and catcalled and had to hear all sorts of ugly things, including tales about her poor Mama. The crowd was going on and on with it. Even those who did not join in seemed to be enjoying the spectacle. Maria literally was a minority of one facing a hostile majority.

Greeks, however, respect courage, even from their worst enemies. When Maria could face them and sing as only she could, the mood changed. She was not only accorded the crowd's tribute for her talent, but for her courage as well. By the second concert, she was as she had always been, Athens' own. Magically, the crisis was over. All that had been like a vote of confidence for the government. The prime minister himself asked Maria to return to Athens, when just weeks before he wished that she never had been born.

All this was not without a price. As soon as she returned to Milan, her personal physician found that she was suffering from nervous exhaustion, and he advised her to cancel any commitments that she had and take a complete rest for at least thirty days.

She was scheduled to perform late that August and the early part of September at La Scala's Edinburgh Festival. Meneghini called Oldani, the general secretary of La Scala, telling him of Maria's condition and of her doctor's advice. He was told that a last-minute change was out of the question. So Maria left for Edinburgh against her doctor's advice. Renata Scotto, a very promising coloratura, was taken along as a possible substitute.

Her première of *La Sonnambula* was broadcast, but she was in bad voice. Her second night went much better, although on her third night she sang so badly that it was almost a disaster. Meneghini blamed her poor performances on the damp, chilly weather, as well as nervous exhaustion. He maintained that after her first night an English doctor had recommended she withdraw. Scotto was hastily called in as her substitute.

By the time they reached London, the English press was already hitting her walkout, saying she had caused another scandal, this time disgracing La Scala. Unwittingly, Elsa Maxwell was to fuel the situation even more.

In Venice, as promised, Maxwell had prepared quite an

elaborate party in Maria's honor. The day Maria arrived, Maxwell had her swamped by the jet set. Maxwell later wrote in her usual gushing narrative that everybody who was anybody was there and that she had never given a better dinner and ball in her life. "I played the piano," she wrote, "and Callas sat on the platform by me humming 'Stormy Weather.' Even two princesses who hated each other were found exchanging smiles while another *comtesse* who wouldn't remain in the same room with Merle Oberon stayed until 5 A.M."

It was interesting how Maxwell, who looked like a tough roly-poly madame of a brothel, considered herself one of two princesses. But it didn't do Maria's Edinburgh walkout much good when Maxwell disclosed, "I have never had a star give up a performance in an opera because she felt she was breaking her word to a friend." It seemed clear to the press that Maria preferred idiotic social parties to sticking to her commitments.

It was at this party that other arrangements, long sought after by Maria, were discussed. Maria was finally to meet Aristotle Onassis, whose ships flew under four flags and whom she called the pirate of the seven seas.

Two days later, the same party-goers went aboard his sumptuous yacht, the *Christina*. Onassis, short and energetic, called Mr. Exuberance by one of the guests, took everyone for the grand tour, showing his El Greco, his collection of Venetian and Byzantine art, the yacht's mosaics and gold faucets, and the lavish, almost obscene bar, with enormous whale teeth and each barstool covered with the foreskin of a whale's copulatory organ. Then he showed them the pool that rose to become a dance floor, and the nine cabins named after Greek islands. But he was especially fond of his El Greco. Now, he said, there were three famous Greeks worthy of some praise aboard his yacht: El Greco, Maria, and, of course, himself.

He expressed that he was only a sailor, completely ignorant of opera, but went into a sort of musical talkathon with Maria about how fond he had always been of the piano. He pointed out that he was so fond of it that he had a grand piano at every one of his villas—some thirty or more—but that did not help his playing.

He then took Maria's hand and kissed it as he had done several times, insisting that he show her his yacht. When she pointed out that he had already done just that, he told her he hadn't shown her nearly everything.

Meneghini was left standing somewhere in the noisy main salon. It was as though he hadn't been there at all.

Twelve

There is a natural built-in envy for one of the richest men in the world. Then, too, it was apparent that Maria preferred the jet set to the opera stage. But Elsa Maxwell may have been doing Maria a disservice by letting forth streams of gushiness about the gay goings on.

A number of things began to happen, seemingly all at the same time, along with an avalanche of some very bitter press. The Edinburgh walkout was followed by Maria's cancellation of an appearance with the San Francisco opera. Her cancellation so infuriated the director that he threw it into arbitration with the American Guild of Musical Artists. Certification of Maria's "nervous condition" did not sit well with anyone, nor was she believed when she regally appeared holding court with jet setters at Lido Beach. The situation was compounded by a rigid week of recording Cherubini's *Medea*, which, it was felt, would have been impossible if Maria were as indisposed as she claimed.

Adding to it, in a series of magazine articles, Renata Tebaldi, took some potshots at her former good friend, Elsa Maxwell. This led to Maxwell's firm reiteration of absolute loyalty to Maria, which really helped to rub everybody the wrong way.

Then, while in New York to appear in court over the disagreeable situation with Eddie Bagarozy, hoping finally to end it, Maria accepted an engagement with the newly formed Dallas

Civic Opera Company. There was already talk in the press that she was going to walk out on that as well and even some speculation that she had lost her voice.

On December 17, just days before she was to leave for Dallas, the press announced that Eddie Baragozy's lawsuit had been settled out of court, although the terms were not made public. Maria stated she was tired of being a courtroom character and very glad the whole boring mess was over and done with.

The bad press kept on even after her Dallas concert, which broke all box-office records. It was billed as a benefit concert, but it seemed Maria was the one who really benefitted, charging such a huge fee that the amount was kept secret.

When Maria returned to Milan, she wasn't exactly welcomed back at La Scala. The Edinburgh Festival was still on everyone's mind. She was accused of disloyalty and having breached her obligation. As was expected, Superintendent Ghiringhelli, who disliked Maria intensely, remained quiet about the situation, when one word from him could have lifted the dilemma.

The feud between Maria and La Scala's superintendent had been building for some time. So when Maria began her November rehearsals for La Scala's 1957-58 season, rehearsing Verdi's *Masked Ball* with Giuseppe di Stefano, Maria was so irritated that her long love duet in the second act was hardly convincing. All the while, she kept her eye on Superintendent Ghiringhelli, as though she were preparing something very special for him.

Just after the 1958 New Year, Maria was to do *Norma*, which Rome audiences had long come to admire. Naturally, the president of the Italian Republic would attend the Rome opening. A substitute for Maria would be totally out of the question. No one could replace her for a night such as this.

Rehearsals had gone very well, and Maria's voice was never better as she sang in full voice for the dress rehearsal, although she was advised to husband her energies. That same evening, she sang on a television broadcast and then celebrated New Year's Eve with friends until after one in the morning.

When Maria awoke that morning, her voice was gone. She could barely whisper. From time to time, she had had a pain in her throat, but never as it was that morning. She clutched her throat and tried to shriek, but all that came out was a hoarse whisper. Turning in her bed, she pounded her pillow and began to cry.

Meneghini was beside himself. He called one doctor after another. None were on call, answering services reminding him that this was the Day of the New Year. He did reach one doctor who told Meneghini that this was the one day he had to remain with his family. Meneghini was willing to pay him anything. The doctor reluctantly told him he would be over to look at Maria, but only briefly.

The same afternoon, the director of the Rome Opera apprehensively came rushing over, and no doubt made the sign of the cross several times. Maria may have looked like Mimi dying, or Cio-Cio-San impaled on the hari-kari dagger. It took only one look at her for the director to be convinced that the gala opening was going to be a disaster. Still, he had to ask how her voice was. Maria whispered hoarsely, "Bad," and was barely able to tell him to get the substitute ready. The director must have said, "Substitute? Impossible!" And he must have thought that this was the gala and the house was sold out.

Maria kept spraying her throat. She would have to go on. The following day, she still had the same pain and hoarseness, even though there had been an improvement earlier. All she faced now was disaster.

The auditorium on the opening night at the Rome Opera was filled to capacity. The première was to be broadcast. She sang, or tried to. What was left of her voice was going fast. She could hardly get through her "Casta diva." Then the first curtain fell, and there were shouts of "Go back to Milan!"

Maria was not coming out for her second act. The conductor, stage director, and the superintendent of the opera all begged her to go on. She just couldn't, she said, and told them to put on a substitute. But there was no substitute.

When the announcement finally came over the PA system that management was suspending the performance—without any sort of explanation other than for reasons beyond their control— it caused a near riot, with fist waving, catcalls, and shouts. A very worried President Gronchi left with the First Lady.

That night, mobs surrounded the Hotel Quirinale, where Maria was staying. The situation continued, worsening the following day with shouts that it was a scandal, Maria was a disgrace, and that she had insulted the head of state. Maria stayed in her suite, along with Meneghini and Elsa Maxwell.

Maria wrote a letter of apology to the president and his wife, and she received a sympathetic phone call from the First Lady. Cables and messages supported Maria with understanding of the situation, but that didn't keep the press from attacking her. To make the situation worse, Maxwell publicly called the Italian press a bunch of barbarians.

All Italy seemed to clamor with the uproar. Italy's honor was at stake. The Rome Opera was to hold another opening with a soprano from Naples named Anita Cerquetti. The Rome Opera needed a triumphant opening of *Norma*. When the final curtain fell, Cerquetti, who was hardly Callas, was brought out for a dozen curtain calls, mainly because she was Italian and Italy's honor had been restored—or at least its citizens hoped it was. There were fervent cries of *"Viva le voci italiane"* and, of course, *"Viva l'Italia!"*

Now, a medical communiqué declared Maria's voice fit, and she was to complete her two remaining performances scheduled for January 8 and 11. The Rome Opera issued their own communiqué, disclaiming any responsibility for Maria's return in light of the present state of tension and possible disturbances which might damage the institution and interfere with law and order. As a result, there was a ruling from the Prefecture of Rome which locked Maria out.

The Italian Parliament heatedly debated *"il caso* Callas," as well as the rivalry and waste of Italian theaters and the excessive power enjoyed by operatic stars. One deputy took on Maria's insult against the head of state, while another deputy went after the Rome Opera management.

Italian editorial writers had a field day. Everyone in opera seemed to have been approached on the subject of *il caso* Callas. Fedora Barbieri, for one, stated that Maria's voice showed strain even during the rehearsals. Meneghini was threatening a lawsuit if Maria was not allowed to return to the Rome Opera. It was more of a threat than anything else. On the morning of January

Thirteen

Three weeks later, Maria stepped out on the stage of the Chicago Civic Opera House to a standing ovation. Afterward, reviewers said that she was in her full glory. However, Roger Dettmer, one of her staunchest supporters, remarked that her voice had aged ten years in one.

Back in New York, she appeared on the TV interview program "Person to Person," with its host, Edward R. Murrow. It was not a very good interview. Murrow may have had a wide range of interests, but opera was not one of them. Basically, what came out of the fifteen-minute program was that Maria was very serious about her art, that she wasn't born in Brooklyn—but it was hastily added that she had friends who came from there—that she was fond of television (when she hated it), and that she seldom went to the movies for fear of catching cold.

The appearance did one thing, though. She didn't come off like a fire-eating monster, and the *New York Herald Tribune* thought she was the "epitome of moderation and easy-going good humor." That she was—eager to please, proud of her art, and eager to return to the Met.

But the whole business of her Metropolitan engagement was up in the air as a result of the head of the San Francisco Opera Company bringing charges against Maria with the American Guild of Musical Artists. An adverse ruling would suspend any and all American engagements.

So, on January 27, 1958, Maria, accompanied by Meneghini, arrived at the Guild's office on Sixtieth Street and Broadway in New York, walking right by an assembly of reporters without talking to them, saying that she would have plenty to say afterward.

The hearing lasted two hours. The board listened to both Maria and Kurt Herbert Adler, who had brought the charges, as well as going over all sorts of voluminous medical evidence that Maria presented.

The board's findings were that Maria had in fact breached her contract by her failure to appear, but it accepted the mitigating circumstances of her ill health as well as her offer to fulfill the second half of her contract. The conclusion was nothing more than a warning, a reprimand for Maria. She was free now to accept her second season with the Metropolitan.

Of three operas, *La Traviata* was chosen for the opening, with some misgivings. The production was almost new, but it had been created for Tebaldi, which Maria could hardly have appreciated. Rather than go into another round of controversy, she felt the wisest thing was to accept the role, although she was not always successful in hiding her annoyance. She had long come to the conclusion that opera directors were all idiots, but she felt Rudolf Bing should have known better.

The night of her second debut with the Met brought on the jitters and a slight pain in her throat, although nothing in the way of shakes. She had a lot of making up to do. Rome had to be a part of the pressures, as well as a great deal more.

When the curtain went up and she emerged as Violetta, the applause was so tumultuous that the performance couldn't even get started. Once it began, Maria earned every bit of the applause. If anyone thought she had lost her voice, they had to be there that night. There rarely if ever has been a more convincing Violetta. She sang as though she was possessed.

Naturally, Elsa Maxwell hailed Maria as *"diva divana,* prima donna of the world," and of course tried to outdo herself with a round of parties. Also, Maxwell single-handedly seemed to fend off Maria's reputation from all attacks.

She wrote in her column, "Why should a woman capable of so noble an expression in the classic arts be tortured by a destiny that makes her happiness almost impossible. Her mother, I believe, without question, has been the cause of this situation."

Whenever the subject of Litza was touched on, Maria, as though she was including all of her friends, would collectively say, "We never discuss my mother."

Other than that, she didn't say anything more, but everyone else did. Elsa Maxwell and her friends got into the act, in addition to all of Maria's friends. Elvira de Hidalgo, who prided herself as Maria's mentor, confidante, and the only important teacher before, during, and after the war, was interviewed quite a few times by *Oggi*, and other Italian magazines.

Maria's sister paraphrased one of Hidalgo's interviews when Jackie wrote, "It seems we dressed luxuriously, very expensively, and we loved to be admired," speaking of herself and Litza. "We never stayed home, always we loved to go out, to dances and theaters, and we made easy friendships, while Maria was shut in the house, deserted, and very poorly dressed. Hidalgo says she took pity on her and tried to teach her not only singing but dress and manners as well. Also she got Maria a position working for Italians to support herself and her family!"

The only position Hidalgo ever got Maria during the war was to teach a pupil who had no real talent, and Maria flatly refused the job. Jackie was the one who was working for the Greek government translating English titles for films. The $6 in drachmas that Maria received for each performance at the Athens Royal Theater could hardly have supported her family, least of all Maria's daily craving for sweets.

The one question I did ask was, How could Maria have gotten so fat if Litza and Jackie were so selfish? Well, I suppose the power of the press makes all things possible, even the impossible.

While all this was going on, Maria let it be known she was on the best of terms with her father, George. She made a point of saying that whenever she was in New York, she would always see him.

Toward the end of February 1958, Maria and George appeared on Hy Gardner's television show. Gardner thought she was a perfectly normal, "nice guy," wondering why he, like so many others, had been influenced by all the bad press stories about her. He found her a warm, sincere, handsome, and down-to-earth human being, "a real live doll."

Maria talked freely about the Rome incident, stating that one of the Rome Opera officials had suggested the collapse during the second act of *Norma* as a dignified way out of the predicament. She also had fine words, although not very accurate, about her husband, stating brightly that it was "love at first sight."

George had little to say in the interview and was embarrassed and ill-at-ease whenever he spoke up. Gardner tried to draw them both out about the dispute Maria had with her mother, Litza. George stiffened, while Maria ignored the issue completely. She did a good job of it, too.

While I was watching the program on the tube, so was Litza.

Back in '51, when Litza returned to the States to sue George for separate maintenance, she lived with Bessie Zarras and her husband in New Brunswick, New Jersey. When she returned in '57 with Jackie, Litza again stayed with Bessie. Then George illegally divorced her in Florida by never bothering to serve her with the necessary papers or telling her about his actions. It was only after some time that he sent her a newspaper clipping about the divorce.

In '58, when Maria appeared on Murrow's "Person to Person," Bessie Zarras decided that the best thing for all concerned would be for Maria to reconcile with her mother. It was an easy matter for Bessie, since she was on speaking terms with Maria, to call her at the Waldorf-Astoria, where she was staying.

Maria was very surprised by the call and sounded very pleasant, asking Bessie where the devil she was calling from.

"New Brunswick," said Bessie. There was a great deal of happy small talk. Then Bessie said, "You'll never guess who I've got standing here with me. Your mother."

There was a long pause. Then Maria asked, "Why? Why do you have her with you?"

"Because we love her."

"You can have her! You can keep her!"

"Oh, you don't mean that."

"Don't I?"

"Your mother only wants to see you. It's the best thing for you. It's the best thing for her. Just give her one hour of your time."

"No!"

"Here, just speak to her. She's right here, waiting. It's the best thing."

"No, never! She's ill, mentally ill. *My God!* Don't you know that?" Then Maria hung up.

Fourteen

When Maria returned to Milan, she found no one had forgotten the Rome Opera *scandalo, disgrazia*. The press was keeping up the attack. Ghiringhelli, La Scala's superintendent, made a point of coldly ignoring Maria completely, either at the theater or whenever they had lunch at the Biffi-Scala, seated at tables just a few feet away from each other. Maria was determined to show him, show them all, with her opening performance of *Anna Bolena*.

On the night of the *première*, scores of Italian police, some two hundred, were at La Scala for the emergency. Everyone was sure something was going to happen. Either Maria would refuse to sing, or someone, quite conceivably, would murder her.

Her first stage entrance was met with absolute silence. When she finished her final curtain, the house nearly came down with the applause. It was like an explosion. As far as anyone was concerned, the Rome Opera walkout wasn't La Scala's business. *La Diva* was superb.

In her dressing room, she was glad her performance was finally over and extremely happy it had gone so well, although she had to be reassured countless times by Meneghini and others that it had. She sat numb and sweating, fanning herself and smiling happily. Now all she looked forward to was a good hot bath and a good night's sleep.

When her chauffeur-driven car turned into the entrance of

her home at Via Buonarroti, it was not apparent that anything was wrong. But in the stark headlights, ghost-like, she first saw it. The entire first floor of her house was covered, even the doors and windows, with human dung, obscene graffiti, and the vilest of naked sexual drawings of Maria, Meneghini, Elsa Maxwell, and Onassis. At first, Maria just stared. Then she screamed and was still screaming when she went into the house, where she vomited.

Meneghini trembled and was so outraged that he was shouting for the servants when he had already dismissed them for the evening. "How could they permit this, *this?*" he shouted. The police didn't sound in the least interested when he hysterically called, as though this sort of thing happened to everyone, that it was an everyday occurrence. This wasn't just anyone, Meneghini shouted, while the policeman on the phone jadedly answered, "Really?"

Meneghini was assured that someone would come to the house, but no one came that night. Meneghini, who had slept little and Maria less, was back on the phone the first thing in the morning.

The police assured him that the matter was not being overlooked and that a car had responded the night before but no one would answer the door. He was told another car would be dispatched to the house. The police who did arrive seemed to find the sight quite enjoyable. Infuriated, Meneghini dashed off a letter to the police chief, citing the incredible indifference, the outrageous conduct, of the Milan police, and demanded that action be taken and protection be provided.

Nothing at all was ever done.

Despite the fact that *Anna Bolena* was given five times at La Scala and was always sold out, rumors persisted that Maria was leaving, never to return, at the end of the season. Early in May, when the final production of Bellini's *Il Pirata* was rehearsed, Maria confirmed what was no surprise to anyone—she would leave after her final performance and return once La Scala was under a different administration.

On that night, she was doing the final scene in *Il Pirata*, when her lover is to be executed and she sees the vision of the scaffold, *il palco*. But another meaning for *palco* is "box seat," and

Maria suddenly zeroed in on just where La Scala's Superintendent Ghiringhelli might be seated, although myopically seeing him only as a blur. Maria sang, but this time with a smile, exercising a very rigid fascist salute in the superintendent's direction. I was quite sure, just as when she had assaulted Alexandria with the spaghetti platter, that she did not drop or waver a single note.

The superintendent quickly retaliated while Maria was taking her final, farewell bows. Amid a standing ovation and banks of flowers descending on the stage, the heavy iron curtain used only for fire emergencies came down suddenly, cutting her off from the audience. It very nearly started a riot. Firemen came out of nowhere and forceably ejected some of the patrons, determined to do the same to the rest of the audience if they didn't leave quietly and quickly.

Maria was later to say to the press, "I take with me the hope to be able to appear again on that stage in the future, under more favorable circumstances."

La Scala's superintendent hinted that the day would come when he would tell his side of the story. He then said, "The prima donnas pass, La Scala remains."

So ended Maria's seven seasons with La Scala.

Rudolf Bing had long been annoyed with Maria. His initial attempted meetings with her, when he first tried to win her over to the Met, did not help matters, and when he saw himself rudely rejected at every turn, no doubt he felt humiliated. Adding to his problems, Maria had left the 1958-1959 Met program schedule pretty much up in the air, other than that she would be there.

Bing wanted her for a series of twenty-six performances in three operas, *Lady Macbeth*, *Tosca*, and either *La Traviata* or *Lucia di Lammermoor*. Clearly, Bing wanted box-office operas, the old warhorses, and was unenthusiastic about Maria's suggestion of forgotten works. So when Maria suggested *Anna Bolena*, Bing dismissed it as an old bore. And the Met schedule was still left up in the air.

The opening of the Met season was only three weeks away when Maria's plane landed at Idlewild International. The Met's projected schedule was for *Lady Macbeth* on February 5, *La Traviata* on the thirteenth and seventeenth, and then *Macbeth* on the twenty-first. What Maria found objectionable was the way they were scheduled. She would have to keep switching her voice back and forth.

This created a critical situation for Bing. He reminded her that it was Met policy to plan months in advance, at the end of every season. Now roles had been assigned, commitments made. Drastic changes at this stage were out of the question. All he could offer her was replacing *La Traviata* with *Lucia di Lammermoor*.

Maria had to wonder if Bing really wanted her to sing at the Met. He was making it impossible. She would have had to been a juggler to pull off *Macbeth* one night and Violetta practically the next. But the vocal gap between *Lucia* and *Macbeth* was even wider, as wide as the Grand Canyon. It would be the same if she were a man asked to sing basso one night and alto-tenor the next. She needed at least three days to bring her voice up or down safely. It would be better for all concerned, particularly for her voice, if she had a "down" schedule for a while, then an "up," not going back and forth, taxing her voice unduly. Bing couldn't alternate the schedule. It was set.

The whole issue was still unsettled when Maria left for a concert tour which the impresario Sol Hurok had arranged, first taking her on a southern tour, then to Canada, and ending with a concert in Dallas. All Bing knew was what he read about her, and I don't imagine it sat well with him when the press printed her statement while with the Dallas Civic Opera she said, "We are doing art."

Bing wired her before her Dallas performance of *La Traviata*, expressing his best wishes, but he also asked, "Why in Dallas?" Maria wouldn't even answer him.

A month later, on November 5, when *Medea* was being given its dress rehearsal in Dallas, Bing wired again. This time, it was an ultimatum demanding that Maria indicate her consent to the Met's schedule no later than November 6, 10:00 A.M., New York time. Maria chose to ignore the message, calling Bing's last wire "Prussian tactics."

The following afternoon, Maria received the final wire, notifying her that her contract with the Metropolitan had been canceled. In a press interview, Bing indicated that he didn't want to get into a public feud with Maria, but that's exactly what he did when he stated, "I doubt if anyone will be surprised at the present turn of events. Although Mme. Callas's artistic qualifications are a matter of violent controversy between her friends and foes, her reputation for projecting her undisputed histrionic talent into her business affairs is a matter of common knowledge.

"This, together with her insistence on a claimed right to alter or abrogate a contract at will or at whim, has finally led to the present situation, merely a repetition of the experience which nearly every major opera house had had in attempting to deal with her. Let us all be grateful that we have had the experience of her artistry for two seasons; for reasons, however, which the musical press and public can well understand, the Metropolitan is nevertheless also grateful that the association is ended.

"The Metropolitan Opera fortunately has never been dependent on the talents, however great, of any individual artist. I could even name a number of very famous singers who thought they were indispensable and would now give their eye teeth to be back with the Metropolitan. So, on with the season."

The dispute was well fueled by Elsa Maxwell and by Maria herself, who expressed bewilderment and fury. She was quite tame when she explained in a television interview that she couldn't switch voices, that her voice was not like an elevator going up and down, and that it was all pretty lousy. But later she exploded, "All those lousy *Traviata*'s he made me sing, without even knowing my partners! Is *that* art?"

In a phone interview with *Oggi* magazine, Maria told of what she viewed as Bing's complete lack of interest for the *bel canto* operas of Bellini, Donizetti, Spontini, Cherubini, and even early Verdi, and what he really wanted, and where it was safe, was the old warhorses. She added that he ran the Met like a Prussian corporal. "For him," she said, "*Macbeth, Lucia, La Sonnambula, Barbiere, Gioconda* can just as well be neatly lined up and placed side by side with the same category of interpretation."

All this created repercussions, with demands for Bing's resignation. Countering were several members of the Met, who supported Bing's position, including Robert Merrill, although he never once appeared with Maria.

But the one thing everyone was asking: Where would she sing next? What was left?

Maria had practically run out of major opera houses in

which to appear. Still, she was getting all sorts of offers from Hollywood and even an offer from Miami Beach for a single appearance during Christmas week. She was deluged with offers.

She did agree to appear in a benefit performance of Bellini's *Il Pirata*, for the American Opera Society in New York, to be held in Carnegie Hall late in January. Parquette tickets were going for $25. I was surprised when I got three tickets in the mail, free parquette tickets that were usually reserved for the press or the elite, the best possible seats. But it wasn't Maria who arranged for them. It was her father. Still, I was pleasantly surprised.

I took my wife and a friend who was a Callas *aficionado*. The opera was in concert form, without scenery, and my friend took quite a number of photos of Maria. At one point, Maria looked down at me, or seemed to, as though she recognized me. I hardly think she saw me, even if she was wearing contacts. She always had a personal way of looking at an audience, picking out one person. It was her way, although she never saw a thing, other than a blur, and preferred it to the sight of someone yawning or scratching his head. My friend was convinced that all was well between Maria and me. He was convinced, but I made no effort to go backstage afterwards. I didn't explain why, other than to say it would be mobbed.

When the reviews came out the following day, some critics actually thanked Rudolf Bing, who never would have programed *Il Pirata* at the Met, for having unwittingly caused this American renaissance of Bellini's long-dormant creation. The comments by Callas *aficionados* were not very complimentary to Bing, and there were many more demands that he be fired.

What followed was that New York City honored its native born. Mayor Robert Wagner read the citation that was presented: "To the esteemed daughter of New York, whose glorious voice and superb artistry have contributed to the pleasure of music lovers everywhere."

My *aficionado* friend wanted to send Maria several of the photos he had taken at Carnegie Hall before she left for Milan. But for some reason, they didn't come out too well. Even though she was in a white gown and wore a long, stagey red stole, her face came out as though she had pimples, the way I remembered her as a young girl, which was very curious.

Fifteen

The first *Medea* at Covent Garden was performed that June 17, 1959, and was attended by members of the Royal Family, Lady Churchill, and all sorts of prominent dignitaries. Also present was Onassis, with his huge entourage of well over thirty guests.

Londoners had not seen Cherubini's *Medea* in nearly ninety years. They weren't prepared for anything like Maria's performance, which overwhelmed them. Her tremendous success called for a celebration by Onassis. He invited nearly two hundred guests, including Lady Churchill, to the Dorchester Hotel to a party whose members reportedly grew into the thousands. It seemed that Onassis had planned the elaborate bash even if her performance had been a disaster. "But, no, it was not," he said. "A better reason to celebrate." Meneghini should have recalled the Latin dictum, "I fear Greeks bringing gifts."

Now it was Maria's turn to be overwhelmed, when all this crush and confusion of thousands of people was in her honor.

Then Onassis invited her, and her husband, of course, aboard the *Christina* for its summer cruise, to go back and forth on the Mediterranean was the way he put it, and he assured them he had plenty of room. Maria had one word, "When?" He told her whenever it was suitable for her. He was quite sure Winston Churchill and Lady Churchill would arrange it for that time as well.

Meneghini had to ask himself what Onassis was up to. He

voiced only that Maria and he were not especially fond of spectacular summers, while Maria said it was a marvelous idea, that it would be great fun. She promised to let Onassis know when she would be free, and she would let him know in a day or two.

When she was to leave with Meneghini, Onassis caught up to them at the elevator, reminding them of his invitation. It looked like a developing tug-of-war, with Maria caught in the middle. Onassis, overly friendly and energetic, was the stronger of the two.

Twice Onassis had his wife, Tina, call Maria about the invitation. Meneghini was running out of excuses. Now it was that his 84-year-old mother was ill, and he was very concerned about her condition. Maria told him that there was nothing he or anyone else could do. He could call his mother—which was about all he could do anyway—from the ship's radio-phone, but she wasn't going to miss that trip for anything.

So on July 22, 1959, they arrived in the principality of Monaco. They could see the *Christina* at anchor out in the harbor—long, white, and beautiful, sparkling in the brilliant sunlight as though haloed with the aurora borealis.

Maria and her husband were met by Onassis and his wife, as well as his sister, Arthemis, whom Maria said she had remembered from before the war in Athens. When Maria asked about Sir Winston and his wife, Onassis said that they would board the following day.

Prince Rainier invited them all to the palace, but Onassis told him another time. Then Rainier reminded Maria that they had the Monte Carlo Opera House, but it badly needed a transfusion. Then he asked if she could possibly consider singing there.

"It's possible," Maria said.

Onassis, smiling—and Maria was later to say that he always smiled like a baboon—asked Maria what it was she had under her arm. She showed him a score of *La Straniera* by Bellini. Onassis asked if she actually expected to study while on board the *Christina,* and told her she must do something totally, completely, absolutely different, that she must free her spirit.

When they boarded the Jacob's ladder of the *Christina,* Onassis wanted to accord the Meneghinis the grand tour. Maria reminded him that he had already done just that on their last visit.

The following morning, after Winston Churchill and his wife were aboard, the *Christina* set out, flying the Liberian flag. Her first ports of call were to be Nice and Genoa. What Maria did not know, nor did any of the guests, was that its forty-odd member crew would often make their peace before boarding her, praying to God they would not run into rough seas, knowing that even a small squall could capsize her.

The *Christina*, no ordinary pleasure craft, measured nearly 350 feet from stem to stern. She had once been the *Stormont*, a war-surplus Canadian frigate, bought from John Shapiro, a Baltimore scrap dealer, for $35,000, and converted in Kiel, Germany, at a cost of over $1.5 million. The German shipbuilder, who had completely refurbished her, warned Onassis against the additional third deck, the hydroplane, and the crane on her midsection. She was top heavy, sluggish, and unpredictable, and could only do 14 knots at best, too slow to maintain her heading in a storm. She was outfitted with heavier engines that got her up to 18 knots, 22 in an emergency, but the ship shook with a constant shudder that had Onassis's El Greco and other fine paintings going askew and nearly falling. He couldn't have that, and had her refitted with her original engines. So this sea butterfly, which was the envy of the world, was actually as practical as a skyscraper built on sand.

Fortunately, the first days were calm. Sir Winston sat in a wide chair on the sunlit varnished deck, wearing a wide-brimmed campaign hat out of the Boer War, smoking an enormously fat cigar. He asked Maria if the cigar bothered her. She replied that she would let him know if it did. When he asked her if she would sing for him and his wife just once, Maria flatly said no, that she didn't feel up to it. All the while, her eyes were on Onassis. And Meneghini was quite aware of it.

Meneghini was all for ending the trip when they anchored off Capri. He was bored with the sensationalism and concerned only with his ailing mother. He showed some annoyance whenever Maria and Onassis spoke Greek, although they occasionally spoke French, of which Meneghini had only some knowledge.

What was obvious to everyone, especially Meneghini,

was the way Maria would always look at Onassis, the way she looked at him the first time Elsa Maxwell introduced them, the way she constantly looked at him at the Dorchester Hotel, and now she couldn't take her eyes off him at all.

Apparently, Meneghini brought this up. Maria told him that his imagination was working overtime, that it was all in his head. She explained that she was only curious about how someone like Onassis could have accounted for such riches, who flaunted it like a little boy with his toys.

Then, when the *Christina* set anchor off Capri, Meneghini felt it was for the best that they both leave. Maria told him she was having too good a time, for the first time in her life, to leave now. Then she added that she was going with Tina and others into town on a shopping spree and that Meneghini could make anything he liked out of that. She kissed him, put on her dark glasses, and left.

The voyage took them to several ports of call, including Piraeus. A brief stopover in Athens, included a trip to the Acropolis. When the voyage continued northeast toward the Dardenelles, the ship ran into rough seas. Except for Onassis and the crew, none of the guests ever knew how dangerous that was. Onassis may have looked like Ulysses, frantically issuing orders, but he was frantic for a very good reason—the instability of his ship in rough water. Maria, though, was greatly impressed with his tone of command without realizing that this was quite necessary. The *Christina* might have gone to the bottom. It was hysterics on Onassis' part more than anything else.

Toward evening, the sea, a cobalt blue, was choppier, spuming splintering pryamidal white caps, clean and brilliant with phosphorescence, while the *Christina* bore anemic lights.

Taking enormous rolls, the *Christina* seemed as though she was going for the bottom when she somehow righted herself. Maria was making her way along the slippery deck with the aid of a safety rope, her reddish hair wet and wild like Medusa's. She managed to scamper back to Onassis' cabin, then to the bridge, the main salon, and to the cargo hold looking for him.

Deep water was in the hold; frantic crewmen were working the pumps; and heavy crates, with broken lashings, were slithering and smashing. Stationed at the steel platform, Maria held on and shouted, asking if anyone had seen Onassis. No one heard her as crates slid and crashed, while one of the ship's officers skipped away, rapidly making the sign of the cross.

She made her way back to the bridge when one of the crewmen said Onassis was there. As usual, Onassis was shouting commands to the bridge. He asked what Maria was doing there. Then he asked where her husband was.

While she stood there, saying nothing, the officers and crew on the bridge pretended to concern themselves with the sea.

Before the *Christina* dropped anchor on August 7, Meneghini apparently knew something had happened. The following day, he was not particularly happy when he and Maria took in the sights of Mount Athos with the Onassis family, or when they were received by the Greek Orthodox Patriarch of Istanbul (formerly Constantinople) who paid tribute to Maria as the world's greatest singer and to Onassis as the greatest seaman of the modern world, the new Ulysses.

That night in their cabin, while Maria and Meneghini were getting ready to attend a party at the Istanbul Hilton, Maria told her husband, very simply, that their marriage was over and that she was in love with Onassis. He probably wanted to kill Onassis. Maria may have laughed and told him that wouldn't be easy. Onassis was nine years younger and a great deal stronger.

When Meneghini pleaded with her, she did tell him if he was going to act like that it was best he stay behind in his cabin. He was still trying to reason with her when she closed the cabin door behind her.

Sixteen

I suppose that after the voyage ended reporters suspected something was wrong when Onassis' personal plane landed at Milan's airport. Meneghini appeared tense, almost stunned. This, however, was accounted for by his concern for his mother.

It was another matter when Onassis turned up at Meneghini's villa at Sirmione, and both Maria and Onassis left hours later. At Via Buonarroti, Maria was in seclusion for days, while Onassis flew back to Venice.

What was first making news in the press was the possible reconciliation between Maria and La Scala. One afternoon, early in September, she drove up to the entrance of La Scala, where she was to do her first run-through of her recording of *La Gioconda*. Everyone was curious about Meneghini being absent. Maria explained that he was staying in Sirmione, to be near his mother, who was still very ill.

Several evenings later, Maria was caught dining at a Milan nightclub with Onassis. The next morning all of Italy knew about it—for that matter, the world—when they were followed until well into the morning, seen entering the Principe e Savoia Hotel arm-in-arm, Maria carrying a bouquet of roses. After that, reporters and photographers besieged the Via Buonarroti. No one could be reached for comment. It became an orgy of speculation.

With all this happening, the press hardly made note of it when, hat in hand, Antonio Ghiringhelli, La Scala's superintendent, and his entire staff greeted Maria in the theater's vestibule.

On September 8, Maria made an announcement to the press, confirming her complete and final break with her husband. She said that it had been in the air for some time, the voyage on the *Christina* being only coincidental, and that the lawyers were working on the case and would be making an announcement. Then she said, "I am now my own manager. I ask for understanding in this painful personal situation. Between Mr. Onassis and myself there exists only a profound friendship that dates back some time. I am also in business connections with him. I have received offers from the Monte Carlo Opera, and there is also a prospect for a film. When I shall have further things to say, I shall do so at the opportune moment, but I do not intend to call a press conference."

Hours later, Meneghini gave his statement, affirming that it was all true. "The separation which means the end of our married life is irrevocable. I do hope that we can reach a mutual agreement without rancor. The causes are very well known, the sentimental link between Maria Callas and Aristotle Onassis. I bear no bitterness toward Maria, who honestly told me the truth, but I cannot forgive Onassis. The laws of hospitality were sacred for the ancient Greeks."

He kept to himself at his villa at Sirmione. The reporters who hounded him were kept at bay. His family, particularly his younger brothers, long alienated because of Maria, reaffirmed their ties. He was even congratulated that he would regain his tranquility.

But he was far from tranquil, bitterly denouncing Onassis: "That man with an ambition like Hitler, who wants to own everything, with his millions and his accursed cruise and his accursed yacht!"

He had, understandably, a mixture of feelings for Maria. He had been loyal and devoted for twelve years and still couldn't believe this event that had wrecked his life. He would sadly say he created her. "She was a fat, clumsily dressed woman, poor like a gypsy, when I met her. And now I hear that I am accused of having exploited her." Now that they would have to divide the community property, he said angrily, "You will see, if everything will be divided, and if we will have to split the poodle, Maria will get the front end and I will end up with the tail!"

Maria's friends saw to it that Meneghini was accused of exploiting her and blamed as the one behind her many problems with La Scala, the Met, and practically everywhere else. Maria was under his influence, they said, and he frequently used poor judgment, and it was his difficulty and not Maria's in getting along with impresarios. It was explained that her reconciliation with La Scala had come about because of her newly gained freedom. With Maria managing her own affairs now, they said, things would be very different.

Reporters found Onassis over at Harry's Bar in Venice, which was once given a good going over by Hemingway. It was Onassis' turn to get a good going over. He didn't mind all the intruding questions at all. He enjoyed them. When he was asked what he thought of his comparison to Hitler, Onassis was delighted when he said, "As you can see, gentlemen, I am a bit shorter, and I don't have a mustache." He expressed pleasure that a woman in the class of Maria Callas was in love with him. "Of course, how can I help but be flattered?" he said. "Who wouldn't be?" But he turned off completely when he was asked what his wife, Tina, thought about all this. When the questions kept on about his wife, he lost his temper.

At a lavish party in Venice given by Elsa Maxwell, Tina Onassis would make no statements whatsoever. Neither would Elsa Maxwell, but she had to feel as though she had been betrayed by Maria.

While Meneghini remained in seclusion at Sirmione, Maria, very business-like, completed her La Scala recording of *La Gioconda*. The next day, Onassis' personal plane met her at Milan's airport, returning her to the *Christina*. Tina Onassis was off in Paris, and there was speculation that she was seeing her lawyers.

Even the world's announcement of the first Russian Sputnik had to compete for the front page. In Italy, it was a handsdown defeat for the Russians. The whole business of Callas, Onassis, and Meneghini was worked over daily, with all sorts of developments, a regular roundelay of speculations. Tina Onassis was going to sue for divorce and that all sorts of sensational aspects of the triangle would come out at the court hearing. Onassis was brazenly flaunting his newest conquest. Then it was asked just who had conquered whom. It was even suggested that the

Sicilian Mafia would kill Onassis, who was out to build a new opera house for Maria. Another report stated that he would finance her first movie, to be one of many.

Cholly Knickerbocker of the *New York Journal-American*, who never liked Maria very much, set off a few barbs of his own in his syndicated column, stating that it was Maria who was keeping the publicity going and that Onassis would not have an easy time losing her. "But I will make a bet," he wrote, "that the future will still find Ari and Tina Onassis together—with Maria singing a loud solo."

While this was going on, Maria cruised the Mediterraean and the Aegean, then once more flew from Athens on Onassis' personal plane to give a concert in Bilboa, Spain. The Bilboa audience gave her a very cold reception, but she dismissed it as a silly little engagement, a remark which was to draw fire from Spain.

After the *Christina* anchored off the Sicilian port of Messina, she posed at the yacht's railing with Onassis. She made the statement to the press, "There is no romance. Mr. Onassis and his wife are my very dear friends. I hope you will not wreck our friendship."

At the same time, Tina Onassis was in New York instituting a divorce action, which set off another round with the press. Two weeks later, Cholly Knickerbocker announced in his column, "The entire Onassis–Callas powder keg will explode when Giovanni Battista Meneghini sues his wife Maria Callas *on moral grounds* in Brescia, Italy. And in Italy this can *result in a jail sentence*. All in all it should make some pretty sensational reading."

To keep her Berlin engagement, Maria asked her lawyers to obtain a postponement and a new date for her Brescia court hearing. When Maria flew back to the States to keep her engagements in Kansas City and Dallas, Elsa Maxwell finally broke her silence.

After two years of gushiness, taking up Maria's banner and probably having been Maria's staunchest and most powerful advocate, Maxwell did a complete turnaround. She wrote about Maria without mentioning her name, saying, "That much-heralded diva arrives in America." This was followed with a conversation she had had a few days earlier with Leonard Bernstein of the New York Philharmonic.

Bernstein asked, "How do you feel about her?"

"I don't feel anything," said Maxwell.

"But you must take some stand."

"Do you mean morally or musically?"

"Both."

"Musically, I can only say she is the greatest artist in the world," she said.

The question of morality was left out. But it was clear that Maria had also lost out as far as Maxwell was concerned. Their two-year friendship of "two princesses" was over.

When Maria's plane landed at New York's Idlewild International that October 27, she took a limousine to La Guardia for her flight to Kansas City. She was greeted by a horde of well over fifty reporters and photographers. She was chic in a tailored suit, her poodle under her arm, and she was very much annoyed, heading for the boarding gate with the swarm following her. The flashbulbs blinded her. The incessant noisy chatter was like a chorus, all at once.

"Do you love Onassis? . . . Will you marry him? . . . What does your husband think of all this? . . . Will you be reconciled? . . . What will happen at the trial? . . . Are you being charged with adultery?"

Looking straight ahead, she mumbled that she hadn't made any plans. She added, "I want to be left alone." Then she shouted, "Get those wires out from under my feet!" Then, "My God, use your heads can't you? Can't you understand? I've got nothing to say to you! Lay off, will you?"

The next day, Cholly Knickerbocker was at it again, criticizing her for the uncooperative manner in which she treated the very reporters to whom she owed so much and the same press which had built her into an international figure.

At the Midland Theater in Kansas City, where Maria was to perform, the police had a phone tip that a bomb had been placed under the stage. This was a white-tie affair, attended by former President Harry S Truman and the governors of Kansas and Missouri.

Maria, who had considerable experience with bombs before, insisted on at least singing her first aria from Mozart's *Don Giovanni* before the police cleared the theater. She was very calm about it and treated the bomb threat as a joke, some crackpot hoax.

When this prestigious audience was ushered out, and the

police conducted a thorough search, it was found, just as she had suspected, to be a hoax. Maria was later presented to Harry S Truman, who no doubt told her of his own daughter's operatic aspirations. Afterward, at a party given in her honor, she danced with all the local millionaires. The press, particularly the *Journal-American*, was later to make it sound as if she capriciously stood up the governors of Missouri and Kansas and 800 of Kansas City's elite. "The temperamental diva was just too tired to attend a champagne reception in her honor," the *Journal* said. "Gov. James T. Blair, his wife, and the wife of Kansas City's Mayor waited in vain for the Great One to appear."

In the course of fifteen days, Maria was to make two appearances in Dallas, concluding with her departure for her separation hearings in Italy. Her first *Lucia* in Dallas was nearly a disaster. There were far too many vocal mishaps, and the difficult high E-flat in the "Mad Scene" was missed altogether. After her curtain, Maria was heard talking to herself, repeating, "I had the note! I had the note! I don't know what happened!"

On November 9, she was back in New York as a stopover before flying on to Italy. She was in a much better mood with reporters. The reason, it turned out, was that while waiting for her plane out, she had phoned Rudolf Bing. She informed the press that peace was restored. Then she was asked the obvious: "Does this mean you'll return to the Met?" She told them, "It's possible. Right now my main concern is the separation trial. There might be too many legal entanglements and complications. I might have to take a long rest." She was very calm when questioned about Onassis. She answered merely, "He is one of my many friends in Europe." Then she went to board the plane.

When Meneghini arrived at Brescia's courthouse, he was cheered by the crowds. Maria, who arrived just afterwards, was accorded a marked contrast of mostly silence. She was the foreign wife who had abandoned her Italian husband for a foreigner.

The property settlement hearing lasted six hours. Maria came out with possession of the Milan townhouse, as well as most of her jewelry. She was assured sole income from all future recording royalties. Paintings and art objects were to be divided, and Maria was to keep both her poodles. Meneghini was to keep his Sirmione villa, as well as his real estate holdings.

Once agreed upon, Meneghini withdrew his original request that the separation be granted through his wife's fault. The decision was arrived at by mutual consent. So the sensational sex scandal that Cholly Knickerbocker and other reporters had foreseen soon evaporated completely.

But Maria's jaunts with Onassis were still in the news. In an interview, her mother announced that Maria would eventually marry Onassis to further her limitless ambition. She was later to be quoted in Hy Gardner's column in New York: "I was the first victim of Maria. Now it is Meneghini. Onassis will be the third."

Book Four

Seventeen

Litza, who was then living in Manhattan, announced that she was doing a biography-autobiography, focusing on Maria. She appeared on several talk shows on radio and television, including the Johnny Carson *Tonight Show*, and was frequently interviewed by members of the local and foreign press, who took her to expensive dinners, looking to rake up new dirt, but usually raking up only the old.

Although she was pictured as the poor, discarded mother, Litza was far from helpless. Those who tried to use her found they were being used instead. Or there were those who wanted to get close to Maria, and this was the next best thing. They were her constant companions, doing all sorts of small favors, and one gave free secretarial service.

I don't recall which show she was on when Jolie Gabor, the mother of Zsa Zsa, came out of the audience and offered her a job at her Madison Avenue store, which sold only cultured pearls.

Litza wasn't faring as well as many might have thought. Her take-home pay from Jolie Gabor's was $41.50 out of a gross weekly pay of $50, which meant, quite simply, that she could not have supported herself. Publicly, Litza called Jolie "the kindest of sorts." I imagine that Jolie got publicity mileage out of that for her store. There, of course, were always the curious who would come in to see the mother of Maria Callas. Possibly their curiosity compelled them to buy something.

The first time I met Jolie Gabor, who was in her seventies, she had just gotten over plastic surgery. Her face was stretched tight and almost a bluish white, and because of the scars behind her earlobes, she wore a kerchief around her head and neck. Her eyes were black and blue, tearing behind dark glasses. She spoke in a quiet, husky voice.

Jolie's husband, a Hungarian in his fifties, tall, in a suit with exaggerated padded shoulders, had all the solemnity of a man in prison. He managed the store. It was a fine store, with cases of cultured pearls on both sides and small, intimate café-like inspection tables and chairs. Business looked quite good. But they were plagued with crank letters every morning. The curious thing was that the letters, anonymous and vile, were all from Hungarians, telling Jolie to take herself and her daughters back to Hungary. There wasn't very much the family could do about it, Litza told me.

Once or twice, Litza ran an errand over to Zsa Zsa at the Hotel Pierre. Naturally, I was curious about what Zsa Zsa was like. Litza's description of Zsa Zsa was interesting. "Little, little eyes," she said. "Wide, wide hips."

One afternoon, Zsa Zsa drove up to her mother's shop in a chauffeured Rolls-Royce for the Christmas party. In person, she could take a little of your breath away. When Litza introduced us, Zsa Zsa took my hand and said, "Madame Callas, how remarkably your nephew resembles Maria."

Litza looked at me as though this was the most incredible thing she had ever heard. "Really?" she said.

Very often, whenever I picked Litza up from work, her pleasant, kind expression would change completely, rigidly extending her hand, palm outward, toward the windows of the store, going, "Nah suh!" It was like an obscenity, but to a Greek it could mean anything. "Ten and ten times!" she would say in Greek, which was really laying it on. You couldn't go any higher than that. Litza never did explain it.

Every Tuesday evening, she went to see her writer, Larry Blochman. She was under contract to do a book for Fleet Publishing. But its editor and advisers were very fearful of Maria or Onassis hitting them with a lawsuit, and so they watered down a great deal of the vitality that Litza had put into her manuscript. The end result was that what was in the book was far kinder than had already been published or said. In fact, Litza was giving me far more interesting accounts of Maria, the war, and what happened afterward, than ever appeared in the book. Litza was obsessed with Maria. She was Litza's main topic. And no wonder. I couldn't help but feel sorry for Litza.

During all this time, she lived in a small, seedy, furnished room off Lexington Avenue, in the Sixties. Her room, for $10 a week, was nothing more than a small bed and bureau, and a glaring light bulb. The one closet was jammed with her clothing, and more was hanging from a clothesline across her room. Her suitcases were piled high along the wall, with stickers from much travel.

Her landlord would not permit her to use the electric iron, smoke in her room, or turn on the light after eleven at night, and she was allowed no visitors. To ensure this, he even had a peephole in the wall to look in on her. His wife, an arthritic cripple, made Litza's life even more miserable.

This was brought to a head when the landlord got a mysterious card from Maria which simply said, "Thank you." He had no idea why Maria had sent it, and although it wasn't Maria's handwriting, probably her secretary's, it had her return address at Via Buonarroti. The landlord was proud for having received it, showing it to everyone. Litza was furious that Maria would thank these people when Maria's dogs lived better. "This is what she thanks these animals for?" she said.

Until then, I would leave Litza off in the downstairs vestibule, and the furthest I had ever gone was to the landlord's door. But when I heard about the peephole and the rest of it, I told her, "You're not staying there another minute."

The landlord tried to stop me, holding his arms straight out across the door frame.

I told him, "Don't be ridiculous."

"You're not coming in here," he said.

"I'm not?"

"This is my house!"

I picked him up by his armpits. He went sprawling across his living room, landing on the sofa. His wife was swinging her cane at me, screaming, *"Police, police!"*

Litza's room was just the way she had described it. She hadn't exaggerated one damned bit. A prison cell would have been better. I got all her things together as fast as I could. The landlord's wife stopped screaming the moment I told her I would have her husband arrested for the peephole. The both of them were just sitting on the sofa, staring, while I got all of Litza's suitcases out of there.

I knew, of course, that meanwhile Jackie had given several recitals in Athens and that in '56 she sang under the assumed name of Elena Montessanto when she made her debut in Vercelli, Italy. She was very reluctant to trade in on Maria's name, and yet she was quite successful according to Litza. But I didn't believe Litza at all at the time when she said Jackie's voice was better than Maria's in *Tosca*. The tape Jackie sent me that year proved me wrong. I was astounded. What was even more incredible was that it had the same sweetness as Tebaldi's voice. A voice like that couldn't be held hidden from the world. I told her so. And I made it my business to do something about it, proud as hell that I could help someone with such a voice.

Jackie's letters were always different from Maria's, a subtler kind, and shy, too, and the curious thing, although her English was quite good, was that she would usually end them, "With sympathy." She had me promise to hold off letting anyone hear her tape, because she didn't feel it was good enough and wanted to make another. I assured her that I wouldn't let the tape out of my sight and would wait for the second tape, but in the meantime I would contact whom I could.

I got immediate responses from Columbia Records, RCA, London, and Decca, all of the managers of the classical sections, and one director, were anxious either to arrange for an audition, or to make test recordings. Some were quite willing to give her living and travel expenses to their nearest recording facilities. What really surprised me was when I got a response from Hurok Attractions, Inc., since Sol Hurok was impresario for Maria's American tours. One of his representatives, Michael Sweeley, wrote me that Mr. Hurok was looking forward to hearing the quality of the tape.

Once I started, Litza picked it up from there. Jackie could have been set up in the finest hotel in New York, could have had the best vocal instructors coaching her, and could have given her first recital at Carnegie Hall. But there were no letters from Jackie and no tape. Finally, Jackie wrote that she was back with her fiancé, Milton, but that he was dying of cancer and she couldn't leave him. She just couldn't think of doing anything now. Eventually, Milton did die.

The pity of it was that it all petered away and the world was deprived of a truly great voice. Perhaps Jackie couldn't bring herself to trade in on Maria's name. Or it might have been that she didn't want to become like Maria. That would have been too high a price to pay.

Litza was quite a charmer and very intelligent. But one thing I thought was damned silly was her belief in the hereafter. Bessie Zarras and Litza would do the *phatoe*, the plate which supposedly spelled out messages from the spirit world.

The *phatoe* is similar to a Ouija board, where a "spirit from the world beyond" controls the fingers applied to the plate, and the plate moves around the alphabetical arrangement, spelling out messages.

Maybe it was ridiculous, but Litza foresaw Maria's future long before Maria ever left Athens after the war. Litza turned over Maria's emptied cup of Turkish coffee, syrupy and clinging, turned it traditionally against the saucer three times and read the initials T.S., which later turned out to be Tullio Serafin. So Litza was prone to giving credence to that sort of thing, and apparently Maria believed in it as well.

In New York, Litza was seeing a mystic by the name of Reverend Brown, who was over on West Seventy-second Street. Litza insisted that I go along with her on one occasion. I thought it was a waste of time but went along anyway just to please her.

Reverend Brown's establishment was up in an office building with a waiting room, before coming into what looked like a church altar with heavy oak benches. The only thing missing was the pulpit and stained glass. A dollar was for general admission. For five dollars, you got a private audience. Reverend Brown was a short, dumpy, middle-aged woman with a shock of coarse hair. She would sit in front, in a high straight-backed wooden chair, much like a throne, squeezing her eyes shut, clutching at her breast with anguish. She could see a man with a great flowing mustache, and, yes, a uniform with all sorts of medals. Litza poked me, whispering, "You see, you see. It's my father."

Litza's father was telling her not to worry, that her book about Maria would be a great success, a great literary triumph, compared only to Dostoevski. Litza was still poking me, her eyes very bright, taking it all in.

When it was over, Litza, quite happy, said to me, "Didn't I tell you? She's marvelous. Oh, I believe in her implicitly. Well, what did you think?"

"Oh, it was fine," I said.

I didn't want to tell her that, to me, this was just a circus sideshow. Mystics clue in on whatever you tell them, whether you realize it or not. With Litza, it would be a lot easier. She was public domain.

"Well, weren't you impressed?" she asked.

"Oh, I'm impressed all right. I suppose there are people who can foresee the future, or look into the past for that matter. But your Reverend Brown isn't one of them."

She couldn't believe that. Reverend Brown was well-respected, highly thought of, and Litza was very emphatic about it.

The notes that Litza would pass on to her writer, Larry Blochman, may have been godawful, but she really had a marvelous way of telling a story. I was so enthralled with some of her stories, particularly about Maria and the war, that I committed them to paper. When Litza passed my composition over to Blochman to see what he thought of it, if he could use it, Blochman said, "Thanks but no thanks. The style is too different." So my first literary efforts were shot down.

I had done a painting of Maria, a scene from *Medea*. I didn't think it was half bad, although the eyes were a little cockeyed. I passed it over to Litza with the suggestion that she use it for the cover. She didn't think it was bad either, but said, "You're not a famous artist." That seemed to make a difference. At least Fleet Publishing did use one of my many photographs of Maria for its cover. So that was something at least.

Because of Reverend Brown, I suppose, Litza was convinced that her book about her daughter would be a literary triumph, and, of course, make a great deal of money. The book had gone through the customary galleys and page proofs and was about to be launched when I got a call from Litza one afternoon at work. It wasn't quite what I had expected.

She started off by screaming that she would never have

anything to do with me again, that I wouldn't even get a copy of her book. She screamed I was a gangster, a thief, a murderer, and a spy for Maria. About all I could say was "Now wait just a goddamned minute" when she hung up in my ear. It turned out that she had made the same accusations to her editor at Fleet, a rather quiet man. He couldn't account for it, and neither could I, but he seemed far more upset about it than I was.

Writers, I was soon to learn, go through hell before their books are published, very often go into hysterics, and do and say some stupid things. I know, because I've been guilty of that, and now I understand exactly what Litza was going through. So much is riding on that one egg in one basket, a very constipated egg that takes forever to launch. But I didn't understand it then and thought she had gone completely mad.

It turned out that all this was the result of another revelation from Reverend Brown. In a moment of anguished mysticism, she had told Litza that her loving nephew and her editor, among others, were actually spies for Maria. Litza had often expressed fondness for her editor.

I felt strange whenever Litza called me after that. She explained it, but she never quite apologized, and I would make all sorts of excuses why I couldn't come to see her. First it was that I was getting a divorce and was going through a trauma. Then I was getting remarried, buying a house way out in Nassau County, and was too tired to see her when I was commuting three hours a day, sometimes even more. If I didn't say that, I said something else. I just couldn't quite bring myself to forgive her.

Litza soon discovered she was not a literary giant after all. The book had been fairly successful, but in terms of money, she made very little. She had already left Jolie Gabor's because her feet would swell, she explained, and her eyes weren't very good any more. She was now living off her unemployment insurance and the kindness of friends, and found it very humiliating.

I hadn't seen her for about a year. But one afternoon toward the middle of May 1961, she called and insisted on seeing me. She said it was very important, that it was urgent, she didn't have to tell me why. The newspapers were filled with it. The *Christina* had anchored in the Hudson River with Onassis and Maria aboard.

Eighteen

*L*itza was living in a furnished apartment that had been converted from a hotel in the West Seventies. It was quite an improvement from her former furnished room. It was a large room and kitchenette, but had that shabby clean look of a hotel. On the sofa bed along the wall were gigantic dolls costumed as Aïda, Carmen, and Tosca. They were a specialty item that she made and had sold in Athens. Now she was hoping to sell them to Bloomingdale's, but they cost nearly as much to manufacture as she could get for them.

She had taken to wearing pince-nez style glasses, but was too embarrassed to wear them in public. She said it made her look like an old lady.

"Sit down, dear boy," she said. "I won't bite you. Are you still angry?"

"No, of course not."

"You got thinner. It's been so long since I've seen you. How is your new wife? Should like to meet her some time. Is she pretty?"

"Very pretty."

"German girl, isn't she? Any children? You haven't started on that, have you?"

"No."

"Don't. It's not worth the trouble. Lovely when they're small, but afterward they throw you out."

I had taken a seat and looked around the room and at the

dolls on the sofa bed. The phone rang, and using her small, polite voice, she said, "Hello? . . . No . . . no, I have nothing to say. . . . Yes, I understand, but you must realize my position. . . . Yes, exactly. . . . Thank you." After she hung up, she said, "What a nuisance. Reporters calling me all day about that animal. If I cared to make a comment about Maria and Mr. Onassis—oh, I have a comment to make. I was hoping that was Mr. Brewster." When I frowned, she told me, "He's with the *Journal-American*, an awfully nice man. I called him."

I didn't have to ask why, but I asked her anyway: "What for?"

"The *Journal-American* is syndicated. It will be all over the country, I'm told. I'm going on welfare."

"Say that again."

"Don't look so shocked. I've been thinking about it for some time. I just don't have any choice. I just received my royalty statement for my book. Thirty-seven dollars. Who can possibly live on that? I've run out of my unemployment benefits. I can't expect my friends to keep supporting me. How does it look, particularly now that the animal is here with Onassis?"

"Particularly."

"Well, what do you think?"

"It'll hit the fan, that's what I think."

Just that afternoon Cholly Knickerbocker of the *Journal-American* had taken the usual potshots, not only at Maria, but also Onassis. The *Christina* was now riding at anchor in the Hudson River, enjoying diplomatic pierage, which meant Onassis didn't have to pay a cent. Knickerbocker wondered what Sir Winston Churchill had to do with diplomatic pierage for the *Christina* when he had only been a brief guest on the yacht some years before.

Now with Litza about to march into the Amsterdam Welfare Station to apply for welfare, followed by a battery of reporters and photographers, it didn't take too much imagination to know exactly what would happen. There was Onassis, one of the richest men in the world, and Maria already reputed to be a millionairess making over $100,000 yearly on recording royalties alone, and her mother compelled to apply for welfare. Well, Litza's timing couldn't have been better. It was perfect. Her father, the colonel, would have been proud of her. She knew exactly the right moment to launch a counter-offensive.

"One thing I have to ask you," I said. "Are they running the story yet?"

"Not until I apply."

"You're sure?"

"Of course."

"Well, it's not only the newspapers that will get after her. The welfare people will. It's the law."

"I don't understand that."

"Never mind. Can you hold off until I try to do something?"

"What can you do?"

"I don't know. But if this ever gets out, you'll never get a dime from Maria."

"I'm not getting anything now."

"If this ever goes through, you're sure of never getting a thing. So give me some time to see what I can work out. Maybe even get Maria to give you something, at least enough to live on. I think the first thing to do is call that reporter. Did you say his name was Brewster?"

"Yes, Mr. Brewster."

"First we have to find out if he's running it," I told her.

What surprised me about my call to the *Journal-American* was that Brewster acted very proper. I had a different opinion of reporters—they would do anything to get a story, or so I thought. Brewster told me that when Mrs. Callas walked into the welfare station, he would be right alongside her, but he wouldn't create the story. He wouldn't write it until such time as it happened. I promised he would be the first to get the story exclusively when Litza decided to take action, but I asked him to keep the story away from Cholly Knickerbocker in the meantime.

The next thing I did was to call Uncle George. He was angry with me as it was for having sided with Litza when I was a Kalogeropoulos, which was the way he put it, and we hadn't talked for over a year. I told him not to hang up on me; I had something very important to tell him that I couldn't tell him over the phone; but it concerned Maria and Litza, and I didn't want it getting in the papers. There would be an explosion if it did, particularly now that Onassis was in town.

George told me that Litza could do anything she wanted. Nothing in this world could hurt Maria. I told him this could, and I had to see him.

"All right," he said.

"I'll be right over," I told him.

I hadn't been to his apartment on West 157th Street for some time, not since he had retired. I was shocked that it had turned into a slum, with garbage all over the place. The elevator was covered with obscene graffiti, either scratched, written in pencil and ink, or painted. It all looked so different that I went to the wrong apartment. A tough black woman came to the door, asking suspiciously, "What you want, boy?"

George's was the next apartment. He led me down the long hall. All the bedroom doors were padlocked. It was as depressing as a cell block. He explained that these were rooms he was renting out, mostly to Puerto Ricans. He still maintained the living room and kitchen. The furnishings had gone very threadbare and seedy.

His only treasures, it seemed, were all of Maria's photographs, a great deal more than I remembered. They covered the walls, even standing on the piano, and the coffee and end tables. One wall by the window was covered with tall plants, all the way to the ceiling.

When I took a seat, George said, "Well?"

I was still looking around. "Has Maria visited you lately?"

"No. What's this about Litza?" he asked.

When I told him, he dismissed it completely and said that Litza was crazy and could do whatever she wanted. I told him he was dead wrong. This would be a catastrophe if it ever got in the papers. I told him I had to see Maria to reason with her.

"Impossible," he said.

"You're not going to talk to her, then?"

"Why should I upset her? Nothing can happen."

"All right," I said.

I got up to leave. He asked if I wanted a little wine. I said no and struck a chord on the piano. The sound was very sour and brassy. "You should get this tuned in case Maria ever comes around. But I doubt if she will."

Christ, I said to myself when I left, he was worse off than Litza. And Maria had publicly called George a wonderful, wonderful father.

There would be no point in wiring Maria. She would ignore the warning completely, just as her father had. The following morning, I lost no time in sending Onassis a wire. It read,

ARISTOTLE ONASSIS

REPORT DELIVERY
PERSONAL DELIVERY ONLY
SS CHRISTINA   YACHT BASIN
WEST 79TH ST

MARIA CALLAS' MOTHER INTENDS TO FILE FOR WELFARE   SHE IS WITHOUT
INCOME OF ANY KIND   GOVERNMENT AGENCIES HANDLING WELFARE TAKE
LEGAL ACTION AGAINST CLOSEST RELATIVE   I AM TRYING TO WITHHOLD THIS
CATASTROPHIC ACTION AGAINST MARIA   MOTHER IS MOST DEFINITE   PLEASE
REPLY

Uncle George liked to take his daily constitutional, replete with gloves, hat, and cane. He would never take the subways, which were detestable and smelly. But that afternoon, without his gloves, hat, or cane, he came all the way down to lower Broadway on the subway, between Waverly and Washington Streets, where I worked. It was inordinately warm for May. It was stifling. He came over to me in the office, mopping his face with a handkerchief, and the black dye was running off his mustache like a wash. "My boy, how could you?" he shouted in Greek. "How could you do such a thing? Mr. Onassis is only a friend! He's not my son-in-law!"

Everyone was looking. I got him right out of there, taking him to a corner luncheonette. He was still going on with it, mopping his face. It seemed I had done a most detestable thing in sending Onassis the wire. "Good God!" he said, making the sign or the cross. "Call her! Call Litza right now! You have to stop her!"

"I already have. But I can't stop her for long," I told him. "What about Maria?"

"She'll talk. I guarantee it."

"Interesting."

"First call your aunt right now. Stop her. She can't possibly go through with this. Tell her I've arranged for you to talk to Maria and Onassis and not to do anything, absolutely nothing until that talk."

"When?"

"Tonight, tomorrow, whenever you want," he said.

"Well, well," I said. "Tomorrow will be fine. Let her sweat a little. Seems everybody's doing that."

Litza was delighted when I called and told her. Still, she couldn't believe it. I told her I would be seeing Maria and Onassis the following afternoon. Litza asked me to watch out for tricks. I told her not to worry. I knew a few tricks of my own. I hadn't exactly led a sheltered life. She asked me what I meant and I told her, "Never mind. Just attribute it to good military training."

I was cocky all right. I had the tiger by the tail—two of them. The trick was letting them go without getting mauled. Well, it's difficult to kill a flea with an atom bomb. I wasn't the one who was vulnerable. They were. So I didn't know why the hell I was so worried. Onassis had only crossed swords with the most powerful people in the world, including the CIA. And then there was Maria.

Nineteen

The *Christina* was anchored out in the Hudson River, long and white in the afternoon sun, neatly profiled against the tall Palisades. The yacht basin at West Seventy-ninth Street seemed deserted except for two policemen. When I came toward them, one jerked his chin at me and asked, "You got business?"

"Yes, sir," I said. "The launch is supposed to meet me at four."

Another man approached us. He was an extremely fat man in a black homburg and a black suit that didn't seem to go with him, and he was holding his heavy briefcase out from his side like ballast.

"Hi, chief," one of the policemen said to him.

The fat man ignored him. He was pacing now over at the wharf, nervously looking at his watch.

The same policeman observed, "Onassis must be putting them through the grinder. He's the third in an hour, nervous in the service. Onassis must be eating them up and spitting them out."

The other policeman didn't appear to be very interested. His only interest, it seemed, was when his tour would end.

From the side of the *Christina*, we could see the launch take a long, wide curve. Spray shot like a speedboat, a high silvery white. Then the launch's speed was cut as she came straight on. As the launch came gurgling into the slip, a seaman stood with a long grappling pole, while a second one came out of the wheel-house as soon as she was tied in. The fat man boarded the launch first, impatiently shaking off the seaman who tried to help him. The second seaman, showing a great deal of gold teeth, asked if I was Meester Linakis.

I nodded and stepped aboard, feeling the slippery sway of the launch. Her deck was a sweat of spray. The launch was nearly as big as a cabin cruiser. The jittery fat man had gone into the wheelhouse, drumming his fingers on his briefcase.

The launch headed out toward the *Christina*, windows wet with spray. The *Christina* was enormous. Sailing nearby were several pleasure craft of all sorts, some with sails. The people aboard were very curious about us. When the launch bumped against the side of the yacht, you could see some people training binoculars on us and some waving when we came out of the wheelhouse. They seemed disappointed that we weren't anyone important.

I had started for the Jacob's ladder when the fat man almost shoved me aside, pushing past me. Before I came topside, I could hear someone shouting at him in Greek in a raspy voice. It was Onassis. He was a small man. The voice didn't go with his stature at all, although I suppose there was truth to the joke that he wasn't so small when he stood on all his money.

He wore those funny but famous sunglasses, and was clad only in a shirt, trousers, and what looked like sandals. His shirt was open at the throat, showing a tuft of gray. Small as he was, he was very intense, calling the fat man a complete imbecile and shouting something about an oil spill that would cost a fortune for the clean up. Apparently, the fat man was a Greek sea captain on one of Onassis' tankers.

Then Onassis turned to me and pleasantly enough said, "Moment," before going right back to yelling at the fat Greek.

Two of the ship's officers, both wearing rows of gold braid on their sleeves, came through a door with a rush of music and chatter. There was quite a party going on. A tall, exotic-looking, limp blonde started out with a cocktail in her hand. Spotting me, she said approvingly, "Oh, my," while her escort jerked her back inside.

The fat man headed away. He looked defeated. Onassis turned to me. You could sense that he was glaring behind his dark glasses. "So you are Mr. Linakis," he said in Greek.

"Yes." I felt damned uncomfortable.

He gave a sudden enthusiastic smile, and then shook hands with me. "So nice of you to come." He frowned as the door opened again, and there was another rush of noise and music. "Parties," he said contemptuously. "I don't like parties. I like to breathe." With everything I knew about him, or thought I knew, that sounded like a complete paradox. He roughly called to one of the ship's officers, "*Ella!* Come! Take Mr. Linakis to a cabin." Then amicably he added, "Preferably one not occupied." He shook hands with me again and said, "First I have some business to attend, before we talk about *our* business." He took the same direction as the Greek captain.

The ship's officer saluted me with two fingers to his cap. "Please," he said in Greek and led me along the varnished curve of the deck. Gray-white seagulls cawed in flight. On a small pleasure craft, a woman stood out by the bow, waving a kerchief. The ship's officer waved back and then quickly stepped out in front of me, opening a cabin door.

Inside, several crewmen were cleaning. One stood near a heavy, ornate desk with a clock and barometer mounted like two ship's wheels. The desk and wall lamps illuminated a portrait of a dark-haired pretty woman, dressed in puffy shoulders and lace. Judging by the hair and dress, I imagined the painting to be circa 1890. The woman had a very delicate face.

The crew was animated, talking and joking with the cabin boy. The officer spoke sternly to them in a dialect I barely understood, telling them to finish up and leave. Two of the crew looked down to their feet as they left. The cabin boy remained, standing self-consciously. The officer told him to make himself useful.

I sat for quite a while, drinking a glass of Greek cognac. I didn't feel particularly comfortable despite all the opulence. The same officer left and came back again. He just stood there, trying not to watch me. Then I heard several people coming along and laughing. There was no mistaking the one laugh that was Maria's, bigger than anyone's. I got right up when the cabin door opened.

Maria stood framed in the doorway, smiling with her mouth and her enormous eyes. Her reddish hair was a little windswept. "Ha, Stephanaki," she said. "You old troublemaker." A tall, white-haired man stood behind her. She elegantly raised her hand to her shoulder allowing him to kiss it. All the while, she was looking at me and smiling. The cabin boy shut the door behind her as she kissed me warmly on both cheeks. Her hand came up with a certain air as she took a seat. "Well," she said, motioning me to sit down, "you write very interesting cables."

Here it comes, I thought.

"Like another drink?" she asked.

"Too early."

"It's never too early," she said. "It's too late." Then she smiled again, her hand working upwards, smoothing out her hair as she turned to the cabin boy. "*Deux* cognac," she told him.

I felt very uncomfortable while the boy served us. I tried to make conversation, telling her that this was the best cognac I had ever tasted, and asked if it was Metaxas.

She shrugged and then said almost facetiously, "The host will be glad to hear it. That's what we're pushing these days, Greek cognac. He'll tell you it's much better than the French. Damned patriotic. Wouldn't think so when he's established residence in Monaco. Tax purposes, Stephanaki. Takes the patriotism out of everything."

"You sound bitter."

Her brows went up. "Do I? Hope you don't hold that against me. Quite enough is, you know."

She waited until the cabin boy left, followed by the officer. The moment they had gone, her face changed completely. Here it really comes, I thought.

"Well, what do we do?" I asked. "Shake hands and come out fighting?"

"You sonofabitch," she said.

"I guess we come out fighting. Listen, Mary—I think I can still call you Mary . . ."

She was shouting now, "What's this about my mother, the lunatic? She's going on welfare? The government will get after me? Well? *Tell me!*"

"Listen, shouting won't help. I'm here for your sake, whether you believe it or not. I was the one who stopped your mother from walking into a welfare station with a slew of reporters. And you know exactly what would have happened. The newspapers would *really* have dragged you over the coals. They would have crucified you. And they'll still do it, if you don't straighten it out right now. Now, do you want to hear my sug-

gestion to avoid all this? You just have to give her enough money
to live on. You have to buy her off."

Her eyes danced. "I wouldn't buy her coffin!" she shouted.
Then in Greek, and it sounded much worse, she shouted, "I
wouldn't even give her the lice off my hair!"

"All right. But if you sent her money, got it around that
you were, wouldn't it change everything?"

"My God, don't you understand what she's done to me?"

"What? What has she done to you?"

"Think!"

"I have, believe me. You're the most famous diva in the entire world. You're here on the *Christina*, *Tina*, or whatever. You're
with one of the richest men in the world. *That's* what people see.
How can you possibly justify your mother's existence, the way
she lives? All that damages you. And don't tell me all this publicity about your mother and you hasn't hurt you. It's ridiculous to
keep a thing like that going. And it'll get worse. If this ever gets
out now, it'll be ruinous for you, and you damned well know it,
otherwise I wouldn't have been invited here. Now, shall we talk
about what we can do about this, and end it once and for all?"

"How much do I have to give that lunatic?"

"That's up to you."

"Ari, Mr. Onassis, suggested a villa, a thousand a month."

"Well, that should do it."

"But will it keep her quiet, or will she be running to reporters every two minutes?"

"Listen, once you settle this, I'm sure that will be the end
of it. It'll be much better for you."

"Will it? Steve, you just don't know what she did. No one
knows."

Just then Onassis came in with that enthusiastic smile, still
with his funny sunglasses, that quick-legged walk of his. Seating
himself on the armrest of her chair, he leaned over and kissed her
on the forehead.

"You just missed it," Maria told him, speaking in Greek.
"Think we've solved everything. He likes your suggestion of a
villa and a thousand a month."

"Really?" Onassis asked, and he smiled. He traced his finger along Maria's cheek and spoke without looking at me. "What
sort of work do you do, Mr. Linakis?"

"I work for an electrical firm, downtown Manhattan."

"Electrician?"

"No, a bookkeeper."

"Really? Imagined you to be more talented than that. Maria tells me that you two grew up together in this city." He made some small talk, asking a few things, determining, I suppose, that I was there more as a friend than an enemy. He would punctuate everything with "Ah." The he asked how serious Maria's mother was.

"Very serious," I told him.

"Well, will you do us all a great favor? Talk to your aunt, give her my suggestion, assure her that I'm quite serious, find out how she wants it arranged with her attorneys, and call me personally in two days."

"She doesn't have a lawyer."

"In that case, you can make all the arrangements. Of course, she has to realize this must be kept out of the newspapers."

"Of course."

We shook hands on it.

"When you call," he said "perhaps I can do something for you. I'm sure there are one or two things I can manage, a little more suitable than a bookkeeper. You should never waste your talents."

He went to the large silver tray on the desk and took the crystal decanter. "It's custom at the conclusion of business," he said.

"He likes your cognac," Maria said.

"Mr. Linakis?" he asked, holding up the decanter.

"Fine. I'll have another."

"Told you he really liked it," said Maria. She was still very upset. She had gone almost giddy. "Shouldn't you give him the grand tour? He's entitled to added privileges, particularly what you keep under lock and key. Steve, haven't you been given the grand tour?"

I looked at her. She was going very giddy, while Onassis smiled tolerantly, passing around the drinks.

"Don't forget," she said to me, "when he shows you his El Greco, ask him how much he paid for it, otherwise he gets very disappointed."

"Come on, darling, drink your drink," Onassis said. "We must get back to our guests."

"It's really very wonderful," she said, still going on with it. "Frustration is what you really get. It's the frustration mill. They buy a little of you at a time until they frustrate you completely and you're scared silly to even open your mouth."

I wasn't sure if she was talking about her stage experiences or those with Onassis.

"There's always one thing we can all do," she said. "We can always jump overboard." She put down her drink, and turned to Onassis. Her voice went hoarse, almost whispering, "Come on, darling."

He kissed her hand. He didn't look at me now. "I'll arrange for the launch," he said.

After they had gone, I kept wondering about all that, all right. The same officer was just outside, waiting. I went back in the launch with the same fat Greek, who smiled to himself at times, and the rest of the time fidgeted.

Twenty

Shortly afterwards, the *Christina* left the country. There was no villa or $1,000 a month for Litza. There was nothing. Nor was I made a better job offer for my many talents. Onassis, not completely unexpectedly, never made himself available.

It was in all the papers that Litza tried to commit suicide, swallowing a bottle of aspirins and barbiturates. The *New York Post* treated it badly, wondering what she was trying to pull. I felt very sad when I visited her in the intensive care unit at Roosevelt Hospital. She looked pale and shriveled in the bed, and rubber tubing ran out of her nose and was taped across her forehead. The white, peeling bed guards were pulled up high. A white screen cut her off from the other patients, mostly blacks. I made Litza one promise: I would do all I could for her. Maria wasn't getting away with this.

I sent Maria her mother's hospital bill, along with a blistering letter telling her that if she did nothing about supporting her mother, I would be the one to see to it that it got in all the papers. "All that business," I wrote, "about your mother forced to go on welfare, and how you and Onassis reneged on it, and your mother almost killing herself as a result of it, should make interesting reading. The newspapers will put you so high up on the cross that the vultures wouldn't even get close to you. So what's it going to be? You've got ten days to straighten it out."

A week later, I got an hysterical call from her father. Maria, it seemed, had called him and was bowing to my demands. She would pay the hospital, but I was to stay completely out of it. Dr. Lantzounis, her godfather, would act as mediator and make all the financial arrangements. But there was to be no villa. Instead of $1,000 a month, Maria agreed to pay her mother $250 a month, which is just about what Litza would have gotten from the welfare people. Still, it was considerably more than Maria had ever given her mother in all those years.

There were conditions. None of this, or anything else, would get into the papers, and Litza would return to Athens. That was the only condition Litza didn't like. She refused to be exiled.

I had nothing to do with my Uncle George after that, and I never saw him again. He eventually returned to Greece, where he died. Nor did I have very much to do with Litza, although I contented myself with the idea that I had gotten something out of the situation for her and that I had been the only one in the world who could twist Maria's tail and get away with it.

From time to time, my wife would see more of my aunt than I did. In fact, I hadn't seen her at all since the business with Maria had been settled. I kept making excuses whenever Litza called. I suppose all that nonsense with Reverend Brown still rubbed me wrong. One day, when Litza called again, I tagged on the excuse that I was writing.

"Really?" she said. "I didn't know you were a writer."

I explained that I had been doing a little writing when she was doing the book on Maria. "You remember," I said, "what I passed on to Blochman. That's what started me."

She sounded worried, "You're not doing a book on Maria, are you?"

"No, no. Quite different."

"Is it a nice love story?"

"Don't know if you can call World War II a love story," I said.

She was very interested, and whenever she called after that she would ask how the book was progressing. "Oh, it's coming fine," I would lie. "Keeps me awfully busy." From the sound of it, I had roughed out a 500-page manuscript. I got quite good at talking about the book, when I hadn't committed even a single word to paper.

One afternoon, she called and said she had marvelous

news. A marvelous man, a marvelous friend of hers, was extremely interested in my book. I caught the name of Oscar Collier, but I wasn't sure whether he was a publisher or a literary agent. She told me to join her on the East Seventies that Monday evening to meet him, and, of course, to bring my manuscript.

Here it was a Friday. I was hung. I'm sure Litza told him I had a 500-page manuscript that was sheer genius. I couldn't very well go empty-handed. So over the weekend I typed out twenty-six pages, which weren't half bad, but I didn't think they were all that good either. Still, it came easily enough. Maria had her traumas. I had mine: World War II.

I suppose I was curious to know if I had anything, but I was just as curious about this Collier. He turned out to be a literary agent who, very impressively, was handling people like James T. Farrell. Collier was tall and looked a great deal like Mayor Lindsay, polished and soft-spoken. He gushed a bit when he greeted my aunt, but he didn't seem all that interested when I was introduced to him. I could just imagine what was going through his mind. Every aunt considers her nephew talented, and Collier would have to go through that bore. I was amused by it all.

Collier was a little cold when he asked me how much of the MS I had.

"What?" I asked.

"Manuscript," he said curtly.

"Oh," I said. "I've roughed out about five hundred. But I've only brought a sample, mainly not to waste your time and to see whether or not I had it."

He took my address and phone number, saying he would get back to me as soon as he read it. Then he was happily talking to Litza again.

Before I ever got home, Collier had called. When I returned his call, the first thing he asked me was, "How much more of this do you have?"

"Why?"

"It's not bad. Quite good, in fact. If the rest is like this, I can sell it tomorrow."

"You kidding me?"

He wasn't in the business of kidding anyone, and he wanted to know when he could see the rest of the MS, amending that by saying, "Manuscript."

The hell of it was that out of a downright lie that grew, I became an author, a rather perverse way of contributing oneself to literature.

Although I have since had some successes and some miserable failures, the curious thing was that Maria would always intrude on my writing. In one of my opuses, she showed up as an actress who came in screaming at the heels of the story. She was so compelling as a fictionalized character that she took center stage and made everyone else come off like complete idiots. So in many ways, I suppose, she had affected me, more than I cared to admit.

Once Maria met Onassis, it appeared that her career was very much on the shelf, although from '61 to '65 she made appearances and recordings, but not at nearly as hectic a pace nor as compulsively as her career had driven her initially. Some said her voice was going. Her recording of Bizet's *Carmen*, as far as I was concerned, was definitive. Risë Stevens' *Carmen* was a Girl Scout by comparison. And that wasn't a rose in Maria's mouth. It was a dagger.

Her appearances in New York were very limited. In May of '62, she sang Bizet's "Habanera" and "Seguidilla" at Madison Square Garden, honoring President Kennedy's forty-fourth birthday. In March of '65, she appeared in two performances of *Tosca* at the Met after she and Bing settled their differences. Since she sang so little, there was quite a fuss. Her stage entrance was met with such a roar that the performance was stopped completely. She used her voice sparingly and was very compact, but in the second act she let off some rough high C's, squealing at the end of "Vissi d'arte."

Her voice was going all right. I don't know what she was going through. I no longer had intelligence sources to tell me what was happening, although I could just imagine what was going on.

Then Onassis got involved with Jackie Kennedy, taking her along with her sister, Lee Radziwill, on the *Christina*; Maria would never quietly accept second best. Maria is reported to have said bitterly, "He's obsessed with famous women. He was obsessed with me because I was famous. Now she and her sister, they have obsessed him, and they are even more famous."

Litza, who was then in Athens, sent off a few barbs of her

own when she was interviewed, stating that Jackie Kennedy's eyes were too far apart, that her hips were too wide, and her legs were not very good, and that she laughed like a lunatic when there was no reason to laugh. It seemed Litza, somewhere, had the inside track. I never did pursue it.

Not surprisingly, when it was announced that Onassis was to marry Jackie Kennedy on his island of Skorpios, Maria, I had heard, had not taken it well at all and there had been quite a confrontation. Maria had thrown more than a dozen glasses at Onassis in a Paris café.

One biographer has since suggested that Maria and Jackie K.O. never met. But knowing Maria, I seriously doubt if that was the case, particularly when Maria was about to be tossed over after having been Onassis' mistress for nine years. Based on everything I knew about her, she would have delivered her usual barbs, and then some. Just as the welfare situation had been kept out of the newspapers, it was quite conceivable that such an encounter, if it ever occurred, was kept hidden as well.

I do know that on the day of the wedding on Skorpios, Maria had several newspapers brought to her, all displaying front-page photos of Onassis and Jackie Kennedy. She ordered them spread out neatly on the floor, then walked all over their faces, cutting the photos to pieces with her heels.

Maria, who had been totally inactive for three years, appeared in a film of *Medea*, a nonsinging role. There was something very symbolic about the film, particularly when you remembered everything she had just gone through.

I suppose everyone knows the Greek legend of Medea, Princess of Colchis, the sorceress, and Jason, who carries off the Golden Fleece and Medea. But when Jason abandons Medea for his new love, she seeks bloody vengeance by killing her own children whom he has fathered and sending her rival a poisoned bridal gown.

Judith Anderson was magnificent in the stage production of *Medea*. Still, she was a poor second to Maria's. As Princess of Colchis, with barbaric ornaments down to her feet, Maria was fury unleashed, cursing, weeping, destroying Creon and his daughter, her own children, and then herself, leaving only Jason and his gold. In a curious way, this really was Maria.

Twenty-One

There was absolutely nothing for two years. Then in 1971, a full page ad in *The New York Times* announced that Maria would be conducting master classes at the Juilliard School of Music on a one-time subscription basis. The fee for Juilliard students would be included in their general tuition. Others were to pay $240 tuition for the entire series.

The ad was sheer genius. The 5:30 P.M. classes made it impossible for most students to attend since it was close to the dinner hour, or some were just coming from their jobs. Many didn't even understand the ad. And many were dubious that she would even show up, since there had been a similar announcement at the Curtis Institute in Philadelphia, and Maria had left after only a few days.

Juilliard's opera theater has a seating capacity of one thousand; there were less than two hundred students at the opening session. Not even in Maria's early career in Athens did she suffer such poor attendance. After classes began, Juilliard compounded the problem even further by refusing to sell additional subscriptions or single tickets, even when there was a clamor. Music students the world over are known to be persistent and inventive, and many got in with counterfeit passes. So, thanks to them, there was a near-capacity audience when the series ended on November 19, 1971.

The following year, Juilliard changed its policy, allowing

the sale of both subscription and single tickets. The second series was to run from February 7 through March 17, 1972. Not only several of my friends, but Maria herself, told me it was like a circus. Half the audience, if not most, were there solely to see Callas of the jet set in action.

She was described, for the most part, as being shy, sincere, and professional. She would usually start off by asking, "Well, who feels like singing?" She would work with five or six students during her two-hour sessions and would not allow applause or any sort of interruptions. Usually, a student would be allowed to sing through an aria, and then very carefully, phrase by phrase, note by note, Maria would coach her student. At first, most were stiff, and ill-at-ease. She would be very patient with them and would often get a student to progress to a state of the art that was considered phenomenal. So it was to Maria's credit, not Juilliard's, who had started it off as a near disaster, that the sessions were a success.

At times, she sang short segments, giving examples. Her voice was described as being down an octave, and she sounded very tired. Others described her as being in excellent voice, beautiful and brilliant. One of the latter, a true Callas *aficionado*, offered to take me along with her, as she had two counterfeit passes. When I declined, she asked, "Are you worried about getting caught?" I said, "No, it's not that at all," and I didn't explain.

I could have attended, but I didn't like the idea that it was a circus and that Maria was on exhibition.

My wife rather naively tried to call Maria on several occasions, but she was never put through to her. I imagine that this was how Maria got my number when she called me that time, insisting that I see her. That was the night in early March, when Maria cancelled her classes because she claimed she was ill, but in reality she was concerned about a possible sequel to her mother's book which might have contained the real truth this time.

As it turned out, a sequel to her mother's book had been published in England. It contained an additional chapter or two by Larry Blochman, but nothing that was in any way damaging. I don't know where Maria got the idea that her mother was finally going to reveal all. Other than that, I never pursued the matter. I suppose I could have, but I didn't.

During June of '73, Maria started up her career again. She was to go on a world tour with the tenor Giuseppe di Stefano, which was to begin in Hamburg, Germany. She was risking everything. Her abilities to sustain long phrases were gone. Everything was gone. The voice that everyone knew no longer existed.

She sang that year in Paris, and the following one at Carnegie Hall in New York. The faithful came, but it was all gone. What saddened me most was when I heard her for the last time. She was singing "O mio babbino caro," which was so poignant, with the feeling only she could bring to it. Yet it wasn't even a shadow of what she once was.

She was to make a tour to Tokyo in '75, but cancelled suddenly. I don't know if Onassis' death had anything to do with it, but she expressed more grief in that one photograph of her after his death than all of Jackie Kennedy's put together.

Toward the end, she stayed away from everyone, even her closest friends. She remained almost a recluse in her Paris apartment until she died on September 16, 1977.

Dorio Soria, who formerly headed Angel Records and who had been a longtime friend, was interviewed by the press afterwards. He told how he had spoken to her on the phone only that past summer and how she had been remote in spirit. When he had asked her what she was doing, she replied in a very flat, dead voice, "Nothing." He concluded, "Without being able to perform, she apparently had nothing left to live for."

As had been her birth, so was her death a subject of controversy. Meneghini made the claim that in 1954 he and Maria had made a reciprocal will in which each appointed the other sole heir, and through his attorneys he sought her entire estate. It was estimated that her total worth was anywhere from $10 to $15 million as a result of several profitable shipping deals with Onassis and her lifetime earnings from opera and concerts. Her royalties from recordings would continue indefinitely.

Litza quite effectively countered Meneghini's claim. Under the Greek law *momimos mira*—legal destiny—only Litza and Maria's sister, Jackie, were entitled to the estate. The will, once found, was to be probated, and at the very least, Litza and Jackie would receive half.

Meneghini was angered, claiming that he alone was entitled to the estate after sacrificing himself and his business for her career. He had managed her career brilliantly, and if it hadn't been for him she would have been a dismal failure. When he first met her, she was depressed to the point of abandoning her career altogether. Then he made acid remarks about Litza to the press. "Maria's mother is really extraordinary," he said. "She has suddenly discovered a great affection for her deceased daughter."

Litza quietly pursued the matter through her Athens attorney, and she was upheld by the French courts. Meneghini then made bitter statements, even about which end of Maria's bed he would get. There, however, were no reports of remorse or grief expressed by him about Maria's death that I saw. In the press reports, he seemed far more concerned with a return on his long-term investment.

Then months after Maria's body had been cremated, the urn containing her ashes was stolen from a Paris cemetery. The urn was recovered several hours later, with some of her ashes missing. Even in death, Maria could not be left in peace.

Epilogue

In remembrance of a truly great singer, Giuseppe Verdi once recalled, "Very great, but not always. At times sublime, at other
times eccentric. Her singing style was not of the purest. The voice
was strident in high notes. In spite of everything, a very great, a
marvelous artist." He had been speaking of Maria Malibran. He
might just as easily have been speaking of Maria Callas.

In her lifetime, Maria restored the true meaning of prima
donna, of *La Diva*, *La Divina*. Opera was no longer to be tolerated
as a costumed concert or the strutting of singers whose acting be-
longed with that of the Keystone Kops. Maria gave opera its
truest meaning. In this century, there has never been a singer
who dominated opera more, who changed its course so completely with revivals of the *bel canto*, for which the great Vladimir
Horowitz has the highest respect. Horowitz has long studied the
singing style of the *bel canto* and has applied it to his art of
playing.

On the day following her death, *New York Times* music critic
Harold C. Schonberg wrote "An Appreciation" for Maria. He was
both sensitive and accurate when he stated, "It was because of
her that the revival of the nineteenth-century *bel canto* operas
started; and in a way, such famous singers as Joan Sutherland,
Beverly Sills, Teresa Berganza and Marilyn Horne are her
children."

Her failings as a human being were many. She was a paradox—courageous, frightened, even terrified, presumptuous and arrogant, and limitlessly ambitious. The greatest paradox was that without all of her failings, Maria would never have become the brilliant artist that she was. She will ultimately be remembered solely for her artistry. She will be remembered throughout this century, into the next, and perhaps even beyond that.

I will always remember her. In my mind, I can still hear her singing, not only when she was the great diva, but struggling, and even before that when she was a very young girl, when her ambition was far greater than her voice.

I can still remember so many things, and like most remembrances will end with only the best. I can still vividly recall rushing to see her off when she was sailing to Italy, where it all started for her, and getting there just as they were calling everyone ashore. Then they were taking the gangway away. And there was Maria at the railing with Louise Caselotti and Nicola Rossi-Lemini. Maria was dressed like Carmen, with a skirt and blouse and something in her hair. The sound of the ship's huge foghorn seemed to fill everything. Louise was trying to bring Maria away from the railing. Maria was still smiling and waving. She was bigger than anyone. Well, she was, she truly was.

Index